KIDWATCHING IN JOSIE'S WORLD

A Study of Children in Homelessness

Neva Ann Medcalf

University Press of America,® Inc.
Lanham · Boulder · New York · Toronto · Plymouth, UK

Dedicated to my mother,
Bernice May.
She told me I could do it.

Contents

Figures and Tables

Acknowledgements

No work of this sort is ever the labor of only one person. This book is no different. This work would not have been possible without the help and encouragement of many, many people. First and foremost, thanks go to Jo Anne and Kenneth Haynes for their enthusiastic encouragement, diligent proofreading, and helpful suggestions for clarity. St. Mary's University supported the work with a Faculty Research Grant. Dean Janet Dizinno, School of Humanities and Social Sciences, and Dean Henry Flores, Graduate School, encouraged and supported the sharing of research findings and the writing of this volume. The students in the Department of Education and the Master of Arts in Reading program who were eager to hear about the research and desirous of becoming better teachers for *all* students were a great encouragement for the writing. Jeff Schomberg and Jason Morales, Faculty Instructional Technology, and Jocelyn Robles, Jennifer Fossett, and Charles Ramirez, Education Department Work Studies, helped immensely with editing, proofreading, and formatting of charts and tables. The research could not have been completed without the gracious help of Caroline Byrd, Blume Academic Librarian. And finally, to *all* my friends and family who continued to urge me to keep working. Thank you more than you will ever know.

Chapter 1
Josie, Me, and Kidwatching Research

Children need people in order to become human . . . . It is primarily through observing, playing, and working with others older and younger than himself that a child discovers both what he can do and who he can become.
Urie Bronfenbrenner[1]

Josie was a sweet, innocent kindergartner, small for her age, with big brown eyes and beautiful bouncing dark curls. She had a smile that lit the room and a contagious giggle. She loved to draw, sing songs, listen to stories, and be held. Josie won my affection and tugged at my heart strings. I was a volunteer part-time teacher's aide in the Kindergarten through Fifth Grade classroom at an emergency shelter for the homeless while gathering qualitative data and information regarding the language development of children living in extreme poverty. That is where I met Josie, her brother and sisters, and many other children. She was *so* cute, *so* eager, *so* excited about life, yet *so* deprived, *so* needy, in such a *desperate* situation. She was a contradiction. She was happy when others in her circumstances are depressed. Her academic achievement was above what might be expected of children with her experiences. She interacted well with her classmates when others were withdrawn or confrontational. She seemed starved for individual attention. She would climb onto my lap and sit for an hour at a time while I read to her. Whenever she wanted to get my attention, she would reach up and put her little hands on each side of my face to make sure that I was looking directly at her before she asked her question. Once, she drew a picture of what she thought my house looked like. It was a picture of a castle and I was the princess. She repeatedly remarked about my white hair and blue eyes and constantly told me she thought I was "so pudie." Had I met Josie in any other classroom, in any other area of the city, I would never have guessed that she was among the homeless and destitute.

Throughout the time of this research study, Josie and her family repeatedly entered and then left the shelter with its classroom and the classroom at the local elementary school because of choices made by the mother. Although I really cared about her and the other children, I felt totally helpless to "fix" the situation, to change their stations in life or circumstances. I felt especially helpless in changing the almost inevitable future they faced. That helpless feeling led me to continue the research into avenues of assistance to improve the education and perhaps the eventual achievement of all children caught in the cycle of extreme poverty.

The research was done by observing in classrooms, on the playground, in the hallways and at the lunchroom table. It took the form of "kidwatching" [2] which is "action research—jotting field notes, gathering data from close observation or interview, and interpreting the scene."[3] This is a well established and most effective method of learning about language growth and development and is a valuable tool for researchers.[4] Listening carefully to what children say and watching what they do reveal stages of development, concepts of oral and written language, linguistic strategies, and uses of language. Observing children in the classroom and in other natural settings indicates things about their language that can be learned in no other way. "We aren't outsiders peering from the shadows into the classroom, but insiders responsible to the students whose learning we document."[5]

When testing young children, Fleischer and Belgredan found that informed and knowledgeable perceptions of those who have direct contact with children are vitally important in any comprehensive evaluation of them.[6] The term "judgment-based assessment" was employed early on by Neisworth and Bagnato to describe more organized activities for information-gathering purposes.[7] Judgment-based assessment collects, structures, and usually quantifies the observations of professionals regarding the characteristics and performance of the child being evaluated. This is *ethnographic* research and is done from the point of view of "a descriptive rather than analytic endeavor."[8]

To obtain reliable and valid information regarding a child's development, early researchers such as Simeonsson, Hunting, and Parse proposed that the insights, knowledge, and judgments of those working directly with the child be given considerable weight.[9] These judgment-based measures made by informed and experienced observers can evaluate wider possibilities and provide opportunities to evaluate subtleties.[10] Sanjek addressed the concern for validity of ethnography and recommended that researchers carefully judge the data they gather to make the appropriate link between the application of theory and their conclusions.[11] All of this develops with depth of experience and over a great deal of time.

Teachers need to know as much as possible about the children they teach in order to plan instructional activities that are beneficial, interesting, and meet individual needs. Assessment of language, literacy, or any other academic endeavor is not an end in itself. The ultimate goal is to help children become lifelong learners. To support them in reaching this goal, teachers must provide consistent attention and support, focus on the positive, ask open-ended questions, listen carefully, and be patient. A major problem is children's lack of motivation to perform in a situation that is uninteresting and/or unfamiliar. Motivation is necessary if children are to attend and fully participate. The context of learning activities must provide wide variety and complex levels of social cognitive skills. There must be strategies that allow children the opportunity to exhibit their full range of competence.[12]

As Church has said,

> [O]bservation and compassion are your most important tools in the classroom . . . watch, listen, and feel where your children are emotionally, socially, and linguistically. . . . By supporting their burgeoning language skills, you'll ensure that you and they thoroughly experience the adventure that lies ahead. [13]

An understanding of this development can ensure that the child has the opportunity and freedom to formulate and express thoughts and ideas and genuinely demonstrate knowledge and ability. Instruction and assessment must allow for judgment-based analysis by professionals working with young children. Careful analytical judgments regarding the quality of each child's behaviors and responses in the context of the whole setting and situation will lead to a much more valid and reliable "picture" of the child's developmental stage and abilities.[14] The main focus of the observations for this research is the language development of children living in extreme poverty. Therefore, kidwatching as qualitative research data gathering was chosen to fit the unique settings of this research study.

This researcher has been an educator for over 40 years, having taught students in all grades, kindergarten through high school. I have taught the children of wealthy parents and the children of migrant workers. In all the years as an educator, informed teacher observation has been a powerful tool for assessment. This experience and practice in doing *informed observation* have served very well in teaching, in supervision of students, and in research with children.

For more than ten years, I worked with homeless *adults* in New Mexico, California, and Texas, helping many parents with admission to shelters, job applications, reading, and Bible studies. It was observed that communication was primarily from the parent *to* the child and consisted of orders, like "sit down," "be quiet," "don't move," "shut up," "no," "don't," "stop," and so forth. The children appeared to be very obedient and extremely non-verbal. Because communication and language skills must be practiced in two-way interactions to be mastered, it was initially believed that the children lacked these skills.

However, as will be shown in Chapter 5, these ideas regarding the children's language skills were proven wrong. When more in-depth observations of the children were begun, especially when they were separated from their parent(s), they were very verbal, displaying skills for more than adequate communication even though their vocabulary was somewhat limited. Observations in the shelter and in the elementary school classrooms in the housing project have broadened, refined, and deepened insights and knowledge. This type of qualitative data has been invaluable in guiding future teachers toward their own understanding of working with children from all walks of life and all socio-economic levels. Many children in our city, our state, and our country are poor and in need of good teachers. Future teachers must not just be *good*; they must be *excellent*. They must be teachers who will make a difference for these children—teachers who will give them hope and a better future.

This work is dedicated to Josie and all the children who find themselves in desperate, dark, deprived circumstances. As Robert Fulghum said, they are in a "mess not of their own making and that they can never clean up."[15] Our society, our schools, and our teachers must work toward giving these young people the tools they need to cope with the world and to change their situation for a brighter future. If these children do not develop these tools before they are adults, they may be destined to remain in the never-ending cycle of poverty, helplessness, hopelessness, and homelessness.

Notes

1. Bronfenbrenner, U. (1970). *Two worlds of childhood: U.S. and U.S.S.R.* New York, NY: Russell Sage Foundation. i.
2. Jaggar, A. (1985). On observing the language learner: Introduction and overview. In Jaggar & Smith-Burke (Eds.), *Observing the language learner*. Newark, DE: International Reading Association and Urbana, IL: National Council of Teachers of English, 1-7.
3. Zeni, J. (1996). A picaresque tale from the land of kidwatching: Teacher research and ethical dilemmas. *The quarterly*. National Writing Project. Retrieved 5/31/06 from http://www.writingproject.org/cs/nwpp/lpt/nwpr/279. 1.
4. Jaggar, A. & Smith-Burke, M.T. (Eds.) (1985). *Observing the language learner*. Newark DE: International Reading Association and Urbana, IL: National Council of Teachers of English.
5. Zeni, 1.
6. Fleischer, K.H., & Belgredan, J.H. (1990). An overview of judgment-based assessment. *Topics in early childhood special education*, 10(3), 13-23.
7. Neisworth, J.T., & Bagnato, S.J. (1988). Assessment in early childhood special education. In Odom and Karnes (Eds.), *Early intervention for infants and children with handicaps*. Baltimore, MD: Brookes, 23-49.
8. Garson, G.D. (2006). *Ethnographic research*. North Carolina State University. Retrieved 6/6/2006 from http://www2.chass.ncsu.edu/garson/PA765/ethno.htm. 1.
9. Simeonsson, R.J.; Huntington, G.S.; & Parse, S.A. (1980). Assessment of children with severe handicaps: Multiple problems—multivariate goals. *Journal of the association for the severely handicapped*, 5(1), 55-72.
10. Simeonsson, R.J.; Huntington, G.S.; Short, R.J.; & Ware, W.B. (1982). The Carolina record of individual behavior: Characteristics of handicapped infants and children. *Topics in early childhood special education*, 2(2), 43-55.
11. Sanjek, R. (1990). On ethnographic validity. *Fieldnotes: The making of anthropology*. Ithaca, NY: Cornell University Press, 385-418.
12. Pellegrini, A.D. (2001). Practitioner review: The role of direct observation in the assessment of young children. *Journal of child psychology and psychiatry and allied disciplines*, 42(7), 861-869.
13. Church, E.B. (2003). Development ages and stages 5 to 6: Say it loud—say it clear. *Scholastic early childhood today*, 17(5), 29.

14.   Medcalf Davenport, N.A. (2003). Questions, answers and wait-time: Implications for readiness testing of young children. *International journal of early years education*, 11(3), Oxford, UK: Carfax Publishing, 245-253.

15.   Fulghum, R. (1988). *It was on fire when I lay down on it*. New York, NY: Ivy Books, 106. Copyright © 1988, 1989 by Robert Fulghum. Used by permission of Villard Books, a division of Random House, Inc.

Chapter 2
Homelessness and the Shelter

Such poverty as we have today in all our great cities degrades the poor, and infects with its degradation the whole neighborhood in which they live. And whatever can degrade a neighborhood can degrade a country and a continent and finally the whole civilized world, which is only a large neighborhood.
George Bernard Shaw[1]

According to the Stewart B. McKinney Act, 42 U.S.C.§11301. et seq., a person is considered homeless who

> lacks a fixed, regular, and adequate nighttime residence and...has a primary nighttime residency that is: (A) a supervised publicly or privately operated shelter designed to provide temporary living accommodations . . . (B) an institution that provides a temporary residence for individuals intended to be institutionalized, or (C) a public or private place not designed for, or ordinarily used as a regular sleeping accommodation for human beings.[2]

The McKinney-Vento Homeless Education Assistance Act of 2001 includes a more comprehensive definition of homelessness. This statute defines *homeless children and youth* as

> individuals who lack a fixed, regular, and adequate nighttime residence. The terms includes: children and youth who are: sharing the housing of other persons due to loss of housing, economic hardship, or a similar reason; living in motels, hotels, trailer parks, or camping grounds due to lack of alternative adequate accommodations; living in emergency or transitional shelters; abandoned in hospitals; or are awaiting foster care placement. Children and youth who have a primary nighttime residence that is a public or private place not designed for, or ordinarily used as, a regular sleeping accommodation for human beings. Children and youth who are living in cars, parks, public spaces, abandoned buildings, substandard housing, bus or train stations, or similar settings.[3]

There are two main categories of homeless persons: the *visible* and the *invisible*. The visible homeless are seen on the street corners with cardboard signs, under the freeway bridges, or on the street seeking a handout, sleeping, or staring into space. Many of these visible homeless are con artists, addicts, alcoholics, mentally disturbed and/or hopeless. Because these are the homeless that are visible, many in society believe that *all* homeless are like them, that *all* are homeless because of their own doing or choosing. However, the fact is, the majority of homeless persons are *invisible*. They are the unseen who have fallen on hard times, and, through circumstances beyond their control, have lost everything. Yet these homeless are often working very hard trying to accumulate enough resources to get their lives back on track, to regain housing and a productive livelihood. Among these invisible are those living with another family, either friends or extended family; those in shelters receiving assistance, training, and support; and the children of these families. Shelters house a significant number of full-time wage earners. A survey of 27 U.S. cities found that more than one in four homeless people are employed.[4] Thus, for many, even hard work provides no escape from this extreme poverty.

One of the reasons that homelessness has not attained high priority for funds and manpower is this disparity between the *societal perception* and the *invisible reality*. It is especially critical for children who are powerless over their circumstances and must cope with life on the street or in a shelter.

"As long as the homeless person with a cardboard sign doesn't stand on *my* street corner, or live under the bridge *I* have to drive over, or accost *me* for a handout, or appear as a child in *my* neighborhood school, I do not have to think about the problem, and I certainly do not have to figure out what to *do* about it." This is the societal attitude displayed across all economic levels, areas of the country, and with various amounts of political power. It seems that no one cares about those who have no political power or voice. Even the charities that reach out to them are often funded with *guilt equity*, meaning, "I give my money so I do not have to get personally involved; someone else will take care of it and I can say I have done my part."

The National Coalition for the Homeless surveyed people who work directly with homeless persons in 147 communities and 42 states, the District of Columbia, and Puerto Rico.[5] They found that "quality of life" laws often specifically target people experiencing homelessness. In February, 2005, the San Antonio City Council passed ordinances aimed at the homeless. The homeless are barred from public camping or sleeping overnight in public places without lawful permission or permits. Camping is defined as storing personal belongings; making campfires; cooking; or using tents, furniture, refuse, packing material, or vehicles for shelter. The homeless are banned from urinating or defecating in public view or on a street, alley, sidewalk, yard, park, building, right-of-way or any other public place. They are barred from asking for money in a public place; on a bus or at a bus stop; within 25 feet of an ATM, entrance of a bank or check-cashing business. It is unlawful to sit or lie down in the city's central business district. Each violation is a Class C misdemeanor, punishable by a fine up to $500. In conjunction with these ordinances, however, the City did not make any provisions for more shelter space or for public or portable toilet facilities. Thus, the City Council made natural and necessary physical actions illegal without providing any acceptable alternatives. With these ordinances, homelessness in San Antonio, as in many cities and towns across the county, was *criminalized*.

> [E]verybody has to be somewhere. These people have no alternatives. If you're hungry, you beg for food. If you're tired, then you sleep wherever you can find a spot. If you're homeless, you have to live somewhere. . . . He doesn't want to be sleeping under a bridge, but everybody's got to sleep somewhere. He's guilty because the city council, in its brilliance, has made it a crime to be homeless. . . . So the guy gets kicked down another notch. He's been arrested, humiliated, fined, punished, and he's supposed to see the error of his ways and go find a home. . . . It's happening in most of our cities. . . . It costs twenty-five percent more per day to keep a person in jail than to provide shelter, food, transportation, and counseling services. . . . Most of the cities . . . waste money by making criminals out of the homeless.[6]

The National Coalition for the Homeless found that there was systematic abuse of the civil rights of the homeless as a strategy to remove them from sight. Nearly all of the communities surveyed lacked enough shelter beds to meet the demand, and subsidized or public housing is not a realistic option for the extremely poor.[7]

According to the United States Bureau of the Census, 11.7 percent of the U.S. population, some 31.1 million people, live in poverty. Although the overall number of people living in poverty has decreased, the number of people living in *extreme* poverty has increased. Thirty-nine percent of all people living in poverty have incomes of less than half the 2003 poverty guideline established by the U.S. Department of Health and Human Services.[8]

An annual national study, *Kids Count Data Book*, tracks children's well-being. In 2003, in the State of Texas, the percentage of poor people exceeded the poverty rate for the nation as a whole. Texans in poverty made up almost one-tenth of the entire nation's poor population. The number of Texans living in poverty was more than 3.1 million, representing 14.9 percent of the state's residents. The 32.9 million poor Americans represented only 11.7 percent of the nation's total population. A higher proportion of Texas children were poor. Over one million Texas children, about 21.1 percent, were estimated to be living in families with incomes below the federal poverty level. In comparison, only 16.3 percent of children in the United States were poor. Poverty is especially concentrated in the Texas-Mexico border region which, as the U.S. Census Bureau determined, includes the very poorest communities in the entire United States.[9] (Figure 2.1)

The Temporary Assistance to Needy Families (TANF) funding represents a critical support for families with financial distress; however, it reaches only a small fraction of children in households with poverty-level incomes. In Bexar-County, in which San Antonio is located, 23 percent of children live in poverty, but only 5 percent receive TANF support. "[C]hildren in families without adequate financial resources often go without basic human needs such as housing, food, and medical care. Such deprivation negatively affects children's academic,

social and emotional well-being, as well as their long-term economic out-
comes."[10]

Figure 2.1

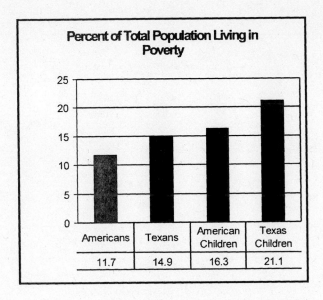

Counting the homeless is extremely difficult due to the very nature of
homelessness. Most studies are limited to counting people who are in shelters or
on the streets. However, these numbers do not begin to include all persons in
extreme poverty and in need of housing. Often, people do not want to be
counted among the homeless so they become very skillful at remaining hidden—living in campgrounds, abandoned buildings, cars, boxes, caves, boxcars,
and other types of hard-to-find and difficult-to-get-to structures and locations.

People who lack a stable, permanent residence have few shelter options because shelters are filled to capacity or are unavailable. A study in 2001 of cities
in the United States found that 37 percent of all requests for emergency shelter
went unmet because of lack of resources. This was a 13 percent increase from
the previous year. For families, the numbers are even worse. There was a 22
percent increase from the previous year, with a denial of 52 percent of emergency shelter requests from families. The number of homeless greatly exceeds
the number of emergency shelter and transitional housing spaces.[11] In the mid-
1990's, families stayed in a shelter an average of five months before moving on
to permanent housing. Today, the average stay is nearly a year.[12]

When the homeless can be counted, research indicates that families, single
mothers, and children make up the largest group.[13] The Urban Institute stated
that 1.35 million children are likely to experience homelessness in a given
year,[14] and the United States Bureau of the Census reported that 40 percent of

persons living in poverty are children.[15] In fact, the 2000 poverty rate of 16.2 percent for children is significantly higher than the poverty rate for any other age group. The Institute for Children in Poverty estimated that *the average age of a homeless person in the United States is 9 years.*[16] "The incidence of poverty among children has increased and become complicated in ways that portend catastrophic consequences, not only for the children themselves, but also for our schools, our economy, and our social well-being."[17] While the homeless are on the *fringe* of society, homeless children are on the *fringe* of *all* support systems, even those designed for the homeless.

Poverty in America knows neither racial nor geographic boundaries. While about two-thirds of poor Americans are white, the rate of poverty is considerably higher for minorities. Four out of nine black children, three out of eight Hispanic children, and 2 out of 11 white children are poor.[18]

Poverty is more than a social label, and it does not operate in isolation. It breeds personal and social disintegration. Difficulties in the areas of health, housing, and education are all linked. The consequences of homelessness severely impact the health and well being of *all* family members. Significant numbers of homeless children suffer a wide range of health disorders and have higher rates of asthma, ear infections, stomach problems, and speech problems. They also experience more mental health problems, such as anxiety, depression, and withdrawal. Hunger and delayed development have potentially devastating consequences if not treated early.[19] In many homeless shelters, infectious diseases like tuberculosis and whooping cough run rampant among youngsters who have not been properly inoculated. "The only common denominator for the children of poverty is that they are brought up under desperate conditions beyond their control—and, for them, the rhetoric of equal opportunity seems a cruel hoax, an impossible dream."[20] Even children living on the *edge* of homelessness lack the stability to make academic success possible.

Parents also suffer the ill effects of homelessness and poverty. Bassuk found mothers in homelessness experienced higher rates of depressive disorders and a significant number had made at least one suicide attempt.[21] Homelessness frequently breaks up families. The stress, feelings of shame, and hopelessness can cause parents to separate, leave their children with other people, or try to disappear from those who know them.[22]

According to Levitas, "There is no grand strategy aimed at eliminating homelessness, no master blueprint on the drawing board of the social engineers. The very complexity of homelessness explains why so many partial 'solutions' are inescapable."[23] James D. Wright, a Tulane University sociologist, said,

> [T]he problem of homelessness is a complex array of many different problems: it is, simultaneously, a housing problem, an employment problem, a demographic problem, a problem of social disaffiliation, a mental health problem, a substance abuse problem, a criminal justice problem, a family violence problem, a problem created by the cutbacks in social welfare spending, a problem resulting from the decay of the traditional nuclear family, and a problem intimately connected to the recent increase in the number of persons living

below the poverty level. No one of these can be singled out as "the" cause of homelessness; probably none of them could even be fairly cited as the single most important factor. They interact in complex ways to produce the homeless problem we confront today. [24]

The most significant piece of federal legislation to address homelessness, the Stewart B. McKinney Homeless Assistance Act, provides many programs for assistance to the homeless. Under this Act, all cities, counties, and states eligible for funds are required to produce a document titled "Comprehensive Homeless Assistance Plan" (CHAP). CHAP must describe need; inventory existing facilities and services; provide a strategy for matching needs with services; account for the needs of targeted groups (homeless families with children, the elderly, the mentally ill, and veterans); and explain how federal funds will aid these efforts.[25]

The emergency homeless shelter in San Antonio, Texas, which was the beginning site for the study upon which this book is based, is a funded center partially operated by the local church community, staffed with both paid and volunteer help. The kitchen is supported by the St. Vincent de Paul ministry. Donations of clothing and personal items are accepted from local churches and charities for distribution among those admitted to the shelter.

Each evening, the homeless line up for a meal and admission to the shelter. Their belongings are searched by the police and only those who have not been using drugs or alcohol are admitted. They are each given a towel, a bar of soap, a toothbrush and toothpaste, and assigned to a bed. The third floor is a large dormitory style room where 118 single men are housed. Families occupy the second floor in 17 small separate rooms with an average of 4 persons each. There are 25 beds for single women in the first floor dormitory room. There are 30 beds reserved for *priority guests* who are allowed extended stays. Priority status is determined by effort made by the homeless individual toward vocational training, high school graduation, and/or employment. While they are making progress, they can remain in the shelter until they have enough resources to move into subsidized housing. There are 9 beds for *Blue Hat workers* who are *priority guests* employed by the shelter. There is an extra room which can be opened in emergencies such as inclement weather which will house an additional 35 people. The average population of the shelter is 250 per night. Church groups come after the evening meal for Bible studies, prayer meetings, and musical performances. There are volunteers who assist with preparation for the GED test which, if passed, can take the place of high school graduation. Other volunteers tutor adults in reading, writing, and life skills.

Although assignment to the shelter is determined one evening at a time, some clients earn the privilege of staying for periods of up to 90 days by working as volunteers in the facility doing laundry, helping in the kitchen, cleaning, doing maintenance, and other such jobs. The length of stay is determined on an individual basis by continuous documented effort by the homeless person toward employment and finding housing. The more diligent clients are allowed to stay longer, since the shelter administration recognizes the effort to improve circumstances and is supportive of those efforts.

Child care is provided to a limited extent for those getting job training or employment. However, the most effective child care in the facility was the kindergarten through fifth grade classroom that was the site of the first phase of this study.

This shelter is where I met Josie and began to appreciate the enormity of the problem of homelessness for her, for her family, and for all the other children like her. I realized that there are vitally important issues that our society *must* address if we are to educate these children, lift them out of poverty, provide for their future, and help them become productive citizens.

Notes

1.   Shaw, G.B. (1971). *The intelligent woman's guide to Socialism, Capitalism, Sovietism and Fascism.* Dublin, Ireland: Penguin Books. Retrieved 12/12/2006 from http://history.eNotes.com/famous-quotes/.

2.   Stewart B. McKinney homeless assistance act (1987). First passed as PL 100-77. Named for U.S. Representative Stewart B. McKinney, Republican from Connecticut, 1.

3.   McKinney-Vento homeless education assistance act of 2001. House Rule 1. Public Law 107-110. Signed into law 1/08/2002, effective 7/01/2002, 2.

4.   United States Conference of Mayors (2001). *A status report on hunger and homelessness in America's cities.* Washington, D.C.

5.   National Coalition for the Homeless (2003). *Illegal to be homeless: The criminalization of homelessness in the United States.* Washington, D.C.

6.   Grisham, J. (1999). *The street lawyer.* New York, NY: Island Books, Published by Dell Publishing a division of Random House, Inc., 205-207.

7.   National Coalition for the Homeless.

8.   United States Bureau of the Census (2001). *Poverty in the United States: Current population reports.* Washington, DC.: Income Statistics Branch.

9.   Center for Public Policy Priorities (2005). The state of Texas children 2005. In *Texas kids count annual data book.* Austin, TX: Texas University.

10.   Ibid., 9.

11.   United States Conference of Mayors.

12.   Santos, F. & Ingrassia, R. (2002). Family surge at shelters. *New York daily news*, August 18, 2002. Retrieved 3/10/04 from www.nationalhomeless.org/housing/familiesarticle.html.

13.   Vissing, Y. (1996). *Out of sight, out of mind: Homeless children and families in small town America.* Lexington, KY: The University Press of Kentucky.

14.   Urban Institute (2000). *A new look at homelessness in America.* Washington, D.C. Retrieved 6/28/06 from www.urban.org

15.   United States Bureau of the Census.

16.   Institute for Children in Poverty (2000). *Who are the homeless?* Poster. New York, NY.

17.   Reed, S. & Sautter, R.C. (1992). Children of poverty. In Kraljic (Ed.) *The homeless problem.* The reference shelf, 64(2). New York, NY: The H.W. Wilson Company, 71.

18. United States Bureau of the Census.

19. Bassuk, E. (1996). The characteristics and needs of sheltered homeless and low-income housed mothers. *Journal of the American medical association*, 276(8), 640-646.

20. Reed & Sautter, 75.

21. Bassuk

22. Shinn, M. & Weitzman, B. (1996). Predictors of homelessness among families in New York City: From shelter request to housing stability. *American journal of public health*, 88, 1651-1657.

23. Levitas, M. (1992). Homeless in America. In Kraljic (Ed.) *The homeless problem*. The reference shelf, 64(2). New York, NY: The H.W. Wilson Company, 13-14.

24. Wright, J.D. (1989). *Address unknown: The homeless in America*. Hawthorne, NY: Aldine de Gruyter Publishing Co., 32-33.

25. Stewart B. McKinney homeless assistance act

Chapter 3
Josie, Her Siblings and Other Children

Poor children live in a particularly dangerous world. . . . It is a world where
even a small child learns to be ashamed of the way he or she lives.
Kenneth Keniston[1]

Josie was a 5-year-old kindergartner in the classroom in the San Antonio shelter
for the homeless. She and her two sisters, Eva and Angela, and her brother,
Jesse, were living in the shelter with their mother who had left an abusive relationship with Josie's father. Eva was in fifth grade, Angela in third, and Jesse
was in second grade. Angela and Jesse had the same father, but different from
either Josie or Eva. I was a volunteer part-time teacher's aide in the classroom
while gathering information and qualitative data regarding the language development of children living in extreme poverty. Josie, her siblings, and the other
children in the classroom were the living faces for the abstract data I had been
studying. Suddenly, I found myself confronted by the reality of what it really
means to be homeless, to be living in a shelter, and to be a member of a misunderstood and unrecognized portion of society. Now, poverty and the harm it
causes for the young and helpless confronted me every day in the lives of these
children that I came to know and care about. It hurt to know there was little I
could do to change their situation. All I could do was try to see that they got the
best teaching and learning experiences possible when I was with them.

Living in poverty exacts a measurable toll on children's overall healthy development. The intellectual, social-emotional, and physical development of
children in low-income families have shown serious negative effect and delay.
In her research for the National Center for Children in Poverty, Gershoff used
three indicators of academic development for children at the end of the kindergarten year. These academic indicators are the main focus of early childhood
education: reading skills, math skills, and general knowledge and understanding
of the world.[2]

Josie was an eager student. She loved to be read to and worked hard at trying to read her favorite stories for herself. She often pretended to "read" these
stories to other kindergartners and was very skillful at retelling stories she had
memorized. She used her finger to follow the text as she "read" and understood
the word-for-word relationship of speech to text. She could recite the alphabet,

but could not consistently identify individual letters when presented randomly. She knew the sounds of some letters and used invented spelling to write notes to her teacher, to the aide, and to me. One of her favorite activities was drawing and she always labeled her pictures. Her math skills consisted primarily of the ability to count to twenty. However, if given the opportunity to use manipulatives such as counting bears, she could figure out simple addition and subtraction problems. She told me, "In Kindergarten, I am learning ABCs and 123s; and soon, when I learned them in English, I forgot them in Spanish. It's easier to say them in English because I forgot the Spanish." Josie and her siblings used English to communicate at all times. They communicated well, even though they had a somewhat limited expressive vocabulary.

Josie's knowledge of the world was limited, as was her expressive vocabulary. She told me about her family. "I've got one sister. She's 8 and my brother is 7. My other sister is some other number I don't know. First I lived far away. Then I went to another place. My mother was trying to get more farther, so she went to Texas. She got a lot of money so she could pay our way here. We had to ride the bus for lots of days because my daddy was trying to find us." I asked how her mother got the money, but she did not know. However, I did learn that they had been in San Antonio about a year.

Angela, the third grade sister, was a very bright, gifted student. She loved to learn new things, solve problems, read, and do art. She was cheerful and excited every day about school and learning. Under other circumstances she might have been in a gifted and talented program leading to Advanced Placement courses and going on to college. With time, good instruction and proper guidance, both Josie and Angela would have been star students. Unfortunately, they were in no position to receive either.

Neither Josie nor Angela was typical of children living in extreme poverty. Others in the classroom were. There was Lorraine, a third grader, who was at least two years below grade level in her reading achievement. Every assignment was a struggle; and, most of the time, Lorraine failed to complete the work because she just gave up in frustration. She said she had been in "lots of schools" because "we have to keep moving because my dad don't have no money for the rent."

Raul, a second grader, was the class clown. However, his acting out was overcompensation for a low self-esteem due to academic failure. He was a nonreader and math was a total mystery for him. "I can't do this papers in school because I never learned how to read so good. My teachers never help me." He, too, had been in "lots of different schools."

Children in low-income families are generally well below average on their reading, math, and general knowledge test scores compared to the well-above-average scores of children living in families with incomes over 300 percent of the Federal Poverty Level (FPL). Only 16 percent of the children in officially poor families scored in the upper range, while over 50 percent of children from the most affluent families did so. Despite these stark differences in average test-performance, it is important to recognize that there is considerable variation in academic achievement *within* each of the groups. The fact that some of the children in low-income families scored considerably above the mean shows that there are children who *are* able to surmount the challenges they face. Determining what enables these children to succeed academically should be an important priority for public policy research.[3] Both Josie and Angela demonstrated achievement above what their living conditions would predict was possible.

Gershoff used four social-emotional development indicators for children at the end of the kindergarten year: social competence; self-regulation; externalizing problem behaviors, such as verbal or physical aggression, poor control of temper, and arguing; and internalizing problem behaviors, such as anxiety, sadness, loneliness or low self-esteem.[4] While development of cognitive skills for achieving academic success is important, it is equally important for children to develop skills to regulate their own emotions and behaviors and interactions with others. The ability to control impulses and to get along with others in early childhood are practice for success in managing the challenges of later life. Shonkoff and Phillips found that problems relating to others such as aggression or defiance, or tendencies to feel anxious or withdrawn can persist into adolescence and can lead to delinquency or risky behaviors such as drug and alcohol abuse and/or suicide.[5]

Jesse, Josie's second grade brother, was a serious discipline problem in the classroom. Although a very competent reader and quite capable in math, he did not *want* to learn. He did not want to participate in class activities. He did not want to do any learning activity. All he seemed interested in was causing trouble. He picked fights with the other boys. He argued with the girls. He bossed everyone around, showed no respect for any adult and refused to obey even the simplest rules of conduct. Jesse gave every indication of being headed for a life of rebellion ending in juvenile delinquency and adult institutions of corrections.

Eva, Josie's fifth grade sister, also exhibited behaviors that indicated problems with self-esteem and proper interactions with others. She already flirted with the men in the shelter. She dressed as provocatively as possible in the hand-me-downs distributed to shelter clients. She acted much older than her 11 years. The last thing on her mind was her school work and studying. She was easily distracted by anything going on around her. She wasted time and seemed unable to start work of her own volition on anything academic. She only engaged in learning activities when an adult–the teacher, aide, or volunteer—worked individually with her. Even then, Eva's full attention was not on learning. "I'm gonna find a rich man and get out of here," she told me one day. Of course, the reality is that Eva was in no position to even be able to meet a "rich man." However, she did appear headed for a life of dependence on men without real regard for the future they could or would offer.

Among all the children, sharing supplies was difficult. The teacher had found that it was necessary to have separate items for each child. She explained that when children have nothing, they tend to become very possessive of the little they do acquire. Therefore, group containers of crayons, paper for shared notebooks, classroom sets of scissors, and so forth were not appreciated or handled well by the children. Every incident of shared usage became a power struggle for "ownership" and control. They did much better when each one had his/her own box of crayons, notebook, and scissors.

The Federal Poverty Level (FPL) is actually insufficient to supply a family's basic needs such as food, housing, health care, child care, transportation, and other necessities. Research has shown a strong pattern of improvement in children's levels of social competence and self-regulation as families' incomes increase.[6] (Figure 3.1)

Figure 3.1 Average Levels of Social Competence and Self-Regulation Within Income-to-Needs Groups, 1998 [7]

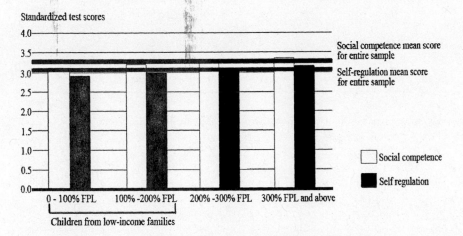

Children from low-income families

In addition, as families' incomes increase, the levels of children's external and internal problem behaviors decrease.[8] (Figure 3.2).

According to Hart-Shegos, homelessness influences every facet of a child's life.[9] It inhibits proper physical, cognitive, social, behavioral and emotional development. During the early years which are critical to development, nearly one-fourth of U.S. children lack medical, nutritional, and early-learning assistance. Many children end up with special needs because of cognitive and developmental problems which could have been prevented by proper prenatal care. Homeless children experience developmental delays that hamper academic success at four times the rate of other children.[10] They suffer from emotional and behavior problems that affect learning at almost three times the rate of other children. Homeless children experience twice the incidence of learning disabilities, such as speech delays and dyslexia, as other children. By the time homeless children reach school, their social, physical and academic lives have been sorely compromised. They are not simply *at risk*; they suffer *severe damage*. Their needs, however, do not lead to greater access to special services. Only thirty-eight percent of homeless children with learning disabilities receive treatment, compared with 75 percent of non-homeless children with disabilities.

Only nine percent of homeless children are in special education classes compared to 24 percent of non-homeless children.[11]

Figure 3.2 Average Levels of Externalizing and Internalizing Behavior Problems Within Income-to-Needs Groups, 1998 [12]

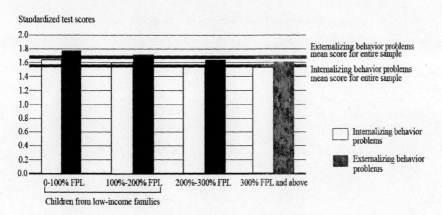

The academic performance of homeless children is hampered not only by poor cognitive development, but by constant mobility. Forty-one percent of homeless children attend two different schools in one year, and 28 percent attend three or more schools.[13] Frequent mobility leads to poor performance and increased behavioral and emotional problems. Mobility also contributes to absenteeism which leads to poor performance which, in turn, can lead to school failure. Grade level retention occurs for some 14 percent of homeless children as compared to only 5 percent of all others.[14]

Differences in test scores are noticeable and consistent. Children in families with incomes below 200 percent of the FPL are well below average in reading, math, and general knowledge. These scores can be compared with the well-above-average scores of children living in families with incomes over 300 percent of the FPL.[15] Thus, academic achievement, social confidence, self-regulation of behavior and general sense of well being are all directly tied to family income level. (Figure 3.3)

Josie had been in two different kindergarten classes in two different states. Eva, Angela, and Jesse had all been in at least four schools that they could remember. Although Angela and Josie seemed to have adjusted very well to their shelter classroom, Eva and Jesse had not. Neither Eva nor Jesse had made friends with classmates and were, in fact, antagonistic and confrontational with them. Neither was achieving academic success or even *trying* to do so. All of the children expressed concern about the possibility of having to change schools again at any time. And indeed, they did have to do that before this research was completed.

Figure 3.3 Average Reading, Math, and General Knowledge Standardized Test Scores Within Income-to-Need Groups, 1998[16]

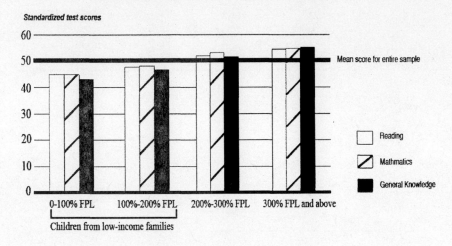

Notes

1.   Keniston, K. (1977). *All our children*. New York, NY: Columbia University Press. The Carnegie Council on Children. Retrieved 12/12/2006 http://education.yahoo.com/reference/quotations/author/Keniston,%20Kenneth.

2.   Gershoff, E. (2003b). Low income and the development of American's kindergartners. *Living at the edge research brief no. 4*. New York, NY: National Center for Children in Poverty, Columbia University Mailman School of Public Health.

3.   Gershoff, E. (2003a). Low income and hardship among America's kindergartners. *Living at the edge research brief no. 3*. New York, NY: National Center for Children in Poverty, Columbia University Mailman School of Public Health.

4.   Gershoff (2003b).

5.   Shonkoff, J.P. & Phillips, D.A. (Eds) & National Research Council and Institute of Medicine. Board on Children, Youth, and Families. Commission on Behavioral and Social Sciences Education (2000). *From neurons to neighborhoods: The science of early childhood development*. Washington, DC: National Academy Press.

6.   Gershoff (2003a).

7.   Ibid., 6.

8.   Ibid.

9.   Hart-Shegos, E. (1999). *Homelessness and its effects on children*. Minneapolis, MN: Family Housing Fund.

10.   Molnar, J.M. (1990). Constantly compromised: The impact of homelessness on children. *Journal of social issues* 46(4), 109-124.

11.   Hart-Shegos.

12.   Gershoff (2003a), 6.

13.   Hart-Shegos

14.   Ibid.

15.   Gershoff (2003a), 5.

16. Ibid.

Chapter 4
Needs, Good Intentions and Realities

Children must be protected not because they are innocent
but because they are powerless.
Mason Cooley[1]

"For the children and youth in poverty, . . . having effective teachers is a matter of life and death. These children have no life options for achieving decent lives other than by experiencing success in school. For them, the stakes involved in schooling are extremely high."[2] "While having the opportunity to enroll and succeed in school may seem like a given to many of us, the McKinney-Vento Homeless Education Assistance Act (2001) was enacted due to the numerous barriers homeless children faced in obtaining a free, appropriate public education."[3] Poverty poses a serious challenge to children's access to quality learning opportunities and to their potential to succeed in school.[4]

Schools should be equipped to help homeless children gain skills to cope with and ultimately to escape from their economic circumstances. But many schools fail many poor children. Poor communities tend to have poor schools as patterns of taxation, lack of parental involvement and political power make a bad situation worse. Educators attempting to meet the educational needs of homeless children must face the reality that, in general, the public school system is not designed to meet these needs. The educational system is designed to serve families living in a much less mobile society. "Assumptions about the nature of children and families that were valid a century ago are no longer relevant; yet, in many instances we have not adjusted our schools to reflect newer realities."[5] Even under the more recent legislative mandates in the McKinney-Vento Act, there are still many gaps between what is required and what is implemented.

There is a lack of understanding on the part of *all* parties when dealing with homeless children. Many homeless students and their families do not understand the schools and social programs. They do not know and/or understand their rights under the McKinney-Vento Act, state laws, and local policies. They do not know how to access necessary services in the community. One of the greatest obstacles impeding the success of homeless students is a lack of advocacy on *anyone's* part. Homelessness equals political powerlessness and voicelessness.

In its report to Congress for fiscal year 2000, the U.S. Department of Education identified a number of barriers that prevent the homeless from enrolling in, attending, and succeeding in school. The Department of Education named immunization requirements, residency requirements, providing birth certificates, legal guardianship requirements, and transportation as the most frequent impediments to ready access to education for the homeless.[6]

School Policies, Practices and Procedures

The first barrier includes school policies, practices and procedures. The average person can not even recognize what can and does pose enrollment and/or attendance barriers for someone who is homeless. What is perfectly fair and appropriate to expect from the average family can pose serious barriers for the homeless that are all but impossible to overcome. Although the McKinney-Vento Act guarantees homeless children the right to immediate enrollment in school, even if lacking paperwork normally required for enrollment, getting a child enrolled in school is very difficult for many. To make sure students enrolling in the school belong in that school, proof of residence is required. This proof may come in the form of a utility bill, rent receipt, driver's license or other documentation. These forms of proof are not possible for the homeless. Requiring emergency contact telephone numbers may not be possible for the homeless parent. Homeless children have trouble with enrollment and admission requirements related to health and inoculation records, proof of residency, guardianship, birth certificates or citizenship. Yet, schools continue to demand those records to complete enrollment of new students. Some parents even believe their children are ineligible to enroll in school because they do not have a permanent residence. The nature of homelessness makes it difficult to obtain records from previous schools for children, and makes it difficult to forward records to schools the children will transfer to when the family is placed in housing. Having the results of testing does not ensure that the student will receive the appropriate follow-up. It is impossible to know whether or not these children have access to the instruction and services that will prepare them for participation in a regular classroom.

These policies and procedures are deeply imbedded by years of established practice. Revising laws and policies to remove these barriers may not be an automatic remedy. The enrollment and admission of homeless children is impeded by school personnel who have not been trained or informed about the legal protections provided to such children under the McKinney-Vento Act and state laws. Training and education of school staff are required to ensure that changes in the law are reflected in daily practices and procedures so homeless students may benefit. School personnel may lack awareness and sensitivity. Sometimes schools are reluctant to enroll homeless students in certain programs or to provide certain services because it is believed that the students will only be in the district for a short time and it is not worth the effort required to enroll them or provide the service. Front office staff are sometimes insensitive to the needs of homeless students, grilling them for answers to common questions: "What is your home phone number?" "Where does your mom/dad work?" "Why didn't you bring a lunch or lunch money?" "Who should we call to come and get you?" All of these questions are legitimate for the average child. They may even be so for the homeless child, but that child has no ready answer and must then reveal what may be considered the shameful family secret that they are indeed homeless.

The McKinney-Vento Act requires that school districts have personnel who are directly responsible for homeless children in their district.[7] Until the passage of this law, school districts had no one person responsible for coordinating programs and ensuring that the needs of homeless students are met. The Act requires districts to keep homeless children in the school they were attending *before* they became homeless. However, this must be requested by the parent or guardian and must be deemed "feasible" by the school district. It requires transportation, tracking, and large budgetary expenditures. Even with homeless program coordinators, many districts find it a daunting task to maintain the necessary records and provide the required services for homeless. Therefore, fulfilling the requirements of the law are deemed "infeasible" and nothing is done.

Mobility

The second barrier to educational access and success is mobility. According to the National Center on Family Homelessness at least 20 percent of homeless children do not attend school at all, while 41percent attend two different schools and 28percent attend three or more different schools during any school year.[8] In her testimony as an expert witness in court cases regarding education of homeless children, Dr. Joy Rogers stated that as a rule of thumb, a student is set back academically by an average of four to six months for each change in schools.[9] The high mobility rate prevents them from receiving appropriate and necessary assessments and referrals to educational programs and services such as special education and gifted and talented programs. These children often do not receive Title I services to which they are entitled. Many children experiencing homelessness are retained in grade or drop out because schools will not provide them the opportunity to make up missed work or regain lost credit as a result of excessive absences caused by frequent moves. Some schools refuse to issue textbooks to homeless students because officials fear that the students will lose the books or fail to return them upon their departure. Sometimes school district policies make it difficult for students to re-enroll by fining them for failing to return equipment or books prior to leaving school. High school students encounter great difficulty accumulating enough credits to qualify for graduation because of their transience, so the dropout rate for these students is disproportionately high. The National Center for Education Statistics found:

> students living in low-income families dropped out of school at six times the
> rate of their peers from high-income families. About 11 percent of students

from low-income families [the lowest 20 percent] dropped out of high school; by comparison, 5 percent of middle-income students and 2 percent of students from high-income families did so.[10]

Transportation

The third barrier for homeless children is the simple matter of transportation for reaching school and maintaining regular attendance. Homeless children often do not receive appropriate educational services and programs because they lack transportation. For students in shelters, or other non-traditional housing, traveling to and from school can pose a tremendous problem. Even if schools are within walking distance for older students, many of the neighborhoods where homeless people find shelter are not safe. Parents are usually reluctant to allow their children to walk to school. The requirements spelled out in the McKinney-Vento Act are that transportation must be requested by the parent or guardian and must be deemed "feasible" by the school district for the student to receive the services. Most homeless parents do not realize that they even have the right to request that their child be taken to another school. Therefore, most homeless children are not transported to the school they were attending before they became homeless. They attend the school that is most convenient to the shelter. Even with these requirements, most states have regulations that may prohibit buses from picking up students who live within a certain distance from the school they attend, often between one and two-and-a-half miles. For financial and other reasons, very few districts provide transportation to students who live outside their district limits or to students living within their district limits who want to attend their prior school when that school is located outside the district limits.

Lack of Home Support for Education

The fourth barrier to school success for homeless children is a lack of home support for education. True readiness for school requires that children be exposed to learning experiences before beginning school and outside of school once they have begun their education. A lack of exposure to learning experiences outside school can be a great barrier to a child's success in the classroom. Children who are homeless often have little or no exposure to activities that stimulate and expand their physical and intellectual development. Because the parents are concerned with basic survival needs, they have little time to devote to activities that develop their children's psycho-motor skills. These students may not have had the opportunity to develop basic study skills or even have an appropriate place to study or do homework. During vacation periods, students with little or no access to educational stimulation lose some of the academic skill gained during the school year. When not in school, there is little opportunity for them to engage in education-related activities and access to books, plays, music, or other arts is severely limited. Through observations and interactions, the author found that homeless children know a great deal about where to get a handout, where to go for a meal, where you can sleep safely, where you can get away with small shoplifted items, when to be noticed and when to be invisible. However, this knowledge does not readily relate to the types of background knowledge expected and even required for making connections with the curriculum of the classroom. Teachers may even be insensitive to this mismatch and make assumptions regarding a student's ability when the problem is actually a lack of background knowledge or school-related experiences.

Health, Safety, Emotional and Social Wellbeing

The fifth barrier is difficulties with health, safety, emotional and social wellbeing. The trauma associated with homelessness makes it difficult for these children to achieve academic success. Maslow's Hierarchy of Needs shows that lower, basic needs must be met *before* academic matters can be taken care of. His five levels of needs are identified as (1) physiological needs, (2) safety needs, (3) belonging and love needs, (4) self-esteem needs, and (5) self-actualization.[11] Maslow emphasized that before higher level needs are even recognized, lower level needs must be satisfied. Poverty and homelessness severely impede the satisfaction of even these basic needs. Schools must ensure that basic health and safety issues are addressed before placing high academic expectations on students in homeless situations. Students may not be concerned about learning math, social studies, or other subject matter when they are preoccupied with how they are going to get their next meal, where they are going to bathe or sleep or get clean clothes, how they are going to get medical and/or dental care. Lack of essential health care may hamper students' ability to attend school. When they attend while suffering health problems, their ability to perform well in school is severely impeded. Many homeless children come to school focused solely on survival and fulfilling their basic needs. Before school personnel can even begin to help these children start the learning process, they must help them meet the basic necessities for survival and well-being.

The author found that most homeless children do not have access to or a means for acquiring clean clothes, items for personal hygiene, or basic school supplies. This causes these children to be embarrassed and reluctant to attend school. They hesitate to make friends or participate in class discussions or other activities. They do not want to draw attention to themselves or their living arrangements, so they become isolated by their situation. Often, these children become close to some individual person, such as a peer or a teacher, only to be yanked away from that person at a moment's notice. They then become even more reluctant to make friends or develop relationships with others for fear they will have to leave that person also. Homeless students are often hurt by non-homeless students making disparaging remarks about clothing, personal hygiene, or living conditions. Students who have been exposed to violent living situations may act aggressively and may not understand how to resolve disputes peacefully. Students with free or reduced cost meal plans are often embarrassed if their meal tickets are distinguishable from other tickets. Students may be embarrassed when they are given a packet of supplies and materials marked for the economically disadvantaged. These students seldom have access to counseling that could help them deal with these stresses. Although there may be exceptions to these observed behaviors and reactions, the problems and needs are very real and must be addressed by our schools.

The need for safety involves more than just security. It includes such things as stability, protection, and freedom from fear and anxiety. Poverty presents the greatest challenge for children in trying to satisfy these needs. Unfortunately, many poor children live in environments that are both unsafe and unhealthy.[12] Longitudinal studies have shown that the mismatch between childhood needs and school expectations leads to long term negative consequences.[13]

> [H]umans are not concerned about satisfying their higher needs . . . until their lower needs...have been met. What this amounts to in the case of students is that they cannot be expected to be interested in learning for learning's sake until they are satisfied that their needs . . . have been met.[14]

The McKinney-Vento Act clearly states that, "State educational agencies (SEAs) must ensure that each homeless child and youth has equal access to the same free, appropriate public education...as other children and youth. . . . In addition, homeless students may not be separated from the mainstream school environment."[15] These students also have the right to all services, including transportation and supplemental services. However, at the time of this study, these regulations were not in effect.

The classroom in the San Antonio shelter for the homeless had been established in 1989 as a remote site of a nearby elementary school under the guidance and authority of the San Antonio Independent School District. It was an old-fashioned one-room school house for students in kindergarten through fifth grade. The district supplied the classroom with textbooks. Older students, 6th through 12th grade, were bussed to nearby middle and high schools.

The classroom was minimally furnished and equipped through the budget of that elementary school. There were no library books, supplementary materials or supplies, videos, tapes, science equipment, educational computer software, overhead projector, or other things that make classrooms adequate learning environments.

The responsibility for the facility was that of the principal and staff of the near-by elementary school and the district support personnel assigned to monitor the schools in the area. The classroom was *supposed* to be supervised by a principal or other administrator of the local elementary school along with the Instructional Steward for the local school district. However, when approached, the Instructional Steward said, "That's not in my job description." The principal said, "I haven't had time to visit the class this year but I've had the vice principal
and the counselor cover it." The vice principal said, "I haven't been to the shelter, but the counselor has." The counselor said, "I haven't been over there

this year, I think the principal does that." The obvious conclusion was that *no one* really had taken responsibility for the quality of instruction taking place in the classroom at the shelter. The principal said, "We used to bring the children over here for P.E., computers and music and things like that, but they got teased by the children here so we just put those things into the shelter school. They get all that stuff there now. We only bring them here for the testing now."

The shelter classroom was staffed by an aide who had been there since its inception and a variety of teachers and substitutes who had stayed for varying periods of time. During the course of this research, the teacher assigned by the district was a high school graduate who had no training of any kind as a teacher. The certified teacher who had originally been assigned to the classroom had resigned due to illness only three weeks after school started in late August. The district had searched for another teacher, but was only able to find this long-term substitute to fill the position. She loved the children, was faithful in her attendance, and tried very hard to do what was needed, but was limited in her effectiveness because of a lack of knowledge and skill.

The lesson plans for the classroom were written by the curriculum specialist at the near-by elementary school and sent over to the shelter via the district delivery service. However, there was no apparent connection between the background and needs of the children and the prescribed curriculum. A great deal of time was spent on worksheets, workbooks, and copying from the chalkboard. The vocabulary/spelling words for the week came from the basal reading text. These were written on the board and the children copied and defined them and then tried to use them in a sentence. One week the words came from a story regarding ballet: "plie," "pointe," "pas de deux," "adagio," "pirouette," "jete," "tutu," and so forth. These were words needed to understand the story, but certainly were not words that children needed to learn to spell and use in independent sentences—especially when they were unable to spell basic words. During this week, the children were studying a unit about the ocean in preparation for a field trip to Sea World. It would have been more appropriate for them to have learned the words associated with that experience.

The worst part was that even when the lesson plans were appropriate, the teacher did not know how to follow them. She was unaware of the basic standards the State had for student learning at each grade level. She knew little about child development, so was unable to provide learning activities at appropriate levels for the children in attendance. Many activities were much too difficult while others were so easy children actually laughed at them. Even kindergarteners were required to copy words from the board, followed by definitions copied from the glossary of the reader. This was extremely difficult for them because of the undeveloped tracking skills and small motor development. Even the teacher's spelling was incorrect on papers and the bulletin boards in the classroom.

The aide primarily worked with the kindergarten and first grade students, while the teacher tried to handle upper elementary. The aide was an Hispanic woman who had worked in the classroom for seven years and for the school district for almost 20. She was looking forward to retirement. She expressed the opinion that she would have been a better teacher for the classroom because she actually had some teacher training and much more classroom experience than the teacher currently assigned to the classroom. However, she said she had learned to distance herself from the children so that she could handle it when they left. So, she was a strong disciplinarian and worked aloofly with the younger students during learning activities.

The question arises as to where the federal funds for these children were being used. They were included in the count of low-income persons for the elementary school. They qualified for free breakfasts and lunches. They qualified for reading remediation funds. They qualified for Head Start and enrichment funds. However, there was no evidence that the monies received by the school for these children were ever actually used to assist them directly.

The children in the shelter were not offered the opportunities to see viable role models for their future. By being confined to the shelter for school and "home" they were only exposed to other homeless persons—adult and children. Although others at the shelter seemed to care a great deal about the children and wanted them to feel loved, this often led to disruption in the classroom. Adults were constantly going by, sticking their heads in the door and speaking or gesturing to the children during lesson time. Over a 4 month period and 100 plus hours of observation time, not a single lesson was completed without interruption. The interruptions were not for *bad* reasons, but the result of people really wanting to help and care for the children. However, these interruptions did keep the children from effective learning and time-on-task. People came into the classroom to help with activities, to give the children all kinds of things from cookies and candy to money. People peeked into the classroom to say "hello" and see how everybody was doing. Staff members and workers came in to get children for paperwork, appointments, counseling, and so forth. This was a case of good intentions leading to negative consequences—the disruption of the learning process. The learning was also interrupted by volunteers to the classroom, parents, clinical staff, shelter staff, and social workers. All these were important people, taking care of important business; however, the result still took away valuable concentration and time-on-task.

The number of children in attendance varied according to the families and single mothers housed in the shelter. The maximum number in the class was 22. During the course of this research, the number ranged from 10 to 18, with an average of 15. There were twice as many girls as boys in the class. Over half were at the kindergarten and first grade level. Only five of the children had no siblings in the classroom. Three of these were only children, while two were the eldest in their families. There were twin girls in the fourth grade who were the aunts of two sisters. Only seven children remained in the classroom for the duration of this research. The remainder of the children either left or entered the shelter while the study was being conducted. Two families entered the shelter during the study, stayed two weeks and left. One was assigned to housing.

Josie's mother met a man in the shelter and they moved out with her four children to "be a real family."

NIMBY (Not In My Back Yard) was and is the attitude of many in response to the needs and circumstances of the children in the shelter. "Intolerance and frustration rather than genuine sympathy and the desire to help have all too often marked public policy in our cities. Genuine efforts at reform are replaced by steps that merely move the homeless out of sight."[16] These children slept, ate, attended school, and received support services within the walls of the shelter. In fact, the only time they even went outside was the 45 minutes they had physical education during the school day. Thus, no one had to see them and be troubled by their existence. However, this meant that the children's experiences were limited and the isolation from the "real world" was almost total.

> It seems we *are* afraid of homeless children. . . . It is hard to know exactly what it is we fear (the children themselves, the sickness they may carry, the adolescents they will soon become if they survive, or the goad to our own conscience that they represent when they are visible, nearby); but the fear is very real. Our treatment of these children reaffirms the distancing that now has taken place. They are not of us. They are "the Other."[17]

The teachers interviewed regarding the best placement for homeless children unanimously agreed that the shelter classroom was the most appropriate. Their reasons included such things as: the children were in a more protected environment in the shelter; they got all the advantages of regular school there without being exposed to criticism from other children; they only stayed in one place for such a short time that it was easier for them if they did not have to try to integrate into a classroom; they had ready access to the social services they needed when at the shelter.

One of the fallacies of these teachers' thinking is that the children suffered isolation. They had no opportunity to interact with other children from diverse circumstances. They lacked opportunities for language and concept development they would have been exposed to when interacting with other children from different environments and backgrounds. Their whole world became the shelter and a very small playground with limited space and equipment surrounded by a ten-foot high wooden fence.

Another fallacy of the teachers' thinking that the shelter classroom was the best place for these children is that the children did not have equivalent opportunities in the shelter that they would have had in a regular school. They did not have music, library, computers, or physical education with qualified teachers.

The shelter library was limited to what had been donated. The music curriculum was not used because no one had the necessary training or skills to implement it. Physical education was supervised by the classroom aide whose only strategy was stretching exercises followed by free play. The computer in the classroom was an old Apple for which there was extremely limited software—

mostly games—and no replacement parts because of the age of the hardware. Neither the teacher nor the aide had computer skills.

The teacher, the aide, and the many volunteers in the shelter classroom all worked very diligently to help the children learn. However, their best efforts fell far short because of the many deficiencies in the existing system. The teacher was untrained and had no guidance. The aide protected herself from emotional attachment. The volunteers came and went without any coordination with the teaching/learning needs and activities. The responsible school failed to fulfill its obligation for supervision and operation. The district failed to meet the requirements of the law for funding, equipping, staffing, and maintaining. The children in this classroom really never had a chance to get an education, improve their lives and pursue their dreams.

Schools must meet the challenges of education for homeless children and must make serious changes in procedures that have been in place for many, many years. The circumstances of the children's lives will not and cannot change to make it easier for the school. The school must change policies, procedures, and assumptions to meet the needs of these children. As Prince and Howard said,

> [A]s a nation the United States is still neglecting to educate properly and care for many of the nation's most vulnerable children, the poor. Despite America's vast wealth, enormous resources, and robust economy, far too many children . . . continue to live disadvantaged lives.[18]

Notes

1.   Cooley, M. (1992). City aphorisms, 10th selection. In Andrews, Biggs, & Seidel (Eds). *The Columbia world of quotations.* New York, NY: Columbia University Press, 2006. eNotes.com. 2006. Retrieved 12/12/2006 from http://history.enotes.com/famous-quotes/

2.   Haberman, M. (1995). *Star teachers of children in poverty.* West Lafayette, IN: Kappa Delta Pi International Honor Society in Education, 1.

3.   National Center for Homeless Education at SERVE (2005). *Homeless education: An introduction to the issues.* Greensboro, NC. Retrieved 10/7/05 from www.serve.org/nche/downloads/briefs/introduction.pdf, 2.

4.   National Center for Education Statistics (1999). *Urban schools: The challenge of location and poverty.* Washington, DC: U.S. Department of Education, Institute of Education Sciences.

5.   James, B.; Lopez, P.; Murdock, B.; Rouse, J.; & Walker, N. (1997). *Pieces of the puzzle.* Austin, TX: STAR (Support for Texas Academic Renewal) Center, 19.

6.   United States Department of Education (2000). *Report to Congress: Barriers to education for the homeless.* Washington, DC.

7.   McKinney-Vento homeless education assistance act of 2001. House Rule 1. Public Law 107-110. Signed into law 1/08/2002, effective 7/01/2002.

8.   National Center on Family Homelessness (1999). *Homeless children: America's new outcasts.* Newton, MA.

9.   Rogers, J. (1991). *Education report of rule 706.* Expert Panel presented in B.H.

v. Johnson, 715 F. Supp. 1387. Illinois.

10. National Center for Education Statistics (2004). *The condition of education 2004*. Washington, D.C.: U.S. Department of Education, Institute of Education Sciences, 61.

11. Maslow, A.H. (1998). *Toward a psychology of being* (3rd Ed.). New York, NY: John Wiley & Sons.

12. National Governors' Association (1992). *Every child ready for school: Report of the action team on school readiness* (Report No. ISBN 1-55877-155-7). Washington, DC: National Governors' Association Publications. (ERIC Document Reproduction Service No. ED 351 125).

13. Finn, J.D. & Cox, D. (1992). Participation and withdrawal among fourth-grade pupils. *American educational research journal*, 29(1), 141-162.

14. Elton, L. (1996). Strategies to enhance student motivation: a conceptual analysis. *Studies in higher education*, 21(1), 58.

15. McKinney-Vento homeless education assistance act of 2001, 2.

16. Kraljic, M.A. (Ed.) (1992). *The homeless problem*. The reference shelf, 64(2). New York, NY: The H.W. Wilson Company, 84.

17. Kozol, J. (1988) *Rachel and her children; Homeless families in America*, New York, NY: Crown Publishers, Inc., 181.

18. Prince, D.L. & Howard, E.M. (2002). Children and their basic needs. *Early childhood education journal*, 30(1), 27.

Chapter 5
Language Development in Daily Interactions

Language is "spiritual food." It is the means by which individuals
share thoughts and feelings.
Dorothy Rubin[1]

The data for this portion of the study were collected over a period of four months with over 100 hours of observation. The research was funded through a Faculty Development Grant from St. Mary's University. Permissions for the study were obtained from the San Antonio Independent School District, the Director of the shelter, the teacher and aide in the classroom, and the parents of the children. No formal testing was done, since instructional time with these children was deemed too precious to be used for that purpose. Natural interactions and language usage were documented while working as a teacher's aide with the students as directed by the teacher and/or regular classroom aide.

Initially, data collection regarding the language development of children in the shelter classroom was done by taping student/researcher, student/student, and student/teacher interactions. However, after approximately 25 hours, it was determined that the presence of the tape recorder was hampering *natural* interactions. Therefore, taping was suspended and data were documented privately.

The researcher had hypothesized that the language of homeless children was deficient in the seven positive indicators of usage as developed by Halliday.[2] These categories are: instrumental language, regulatory language, interactional language, personal language, imaginative language, heuristic language, and informative language. It was also hypothesized that their language was qualitatively below the Standard English used in schools. These hypotheses had been formed over a period of more than ten years of work with homeless *adults* in New Mexico, California, and Texas and casually observing their children interact with them. Observed communication was primarily unidirectional—from the parent to the child—and consisted of orders: "Sit down," "Don't move," Stay there," "Shut up," and so forth. The children appeared to be extremely nonverbal. Research has shown that communication skills do not develop in such an environment. Good communication skills develop when they can be practiced in two-way interactions. Kenneth Goodman stated,

> Language is social as well as personal; it is learned in the process of its social use. Thus parents, caregivers, siblings, peers, and others with whom the developing infant interacts play vital roles in the infant's linguistic development. They are less teachers than essential communicative partners, less role models than respondents, less to be imitated than to be understanding and understood.[3]

Therefore, as stated in Chapter 1, it was hypothesized that homeless children were deficient in language development and communication skills. However, direct observation of these children, especially when removed from the presence of their parents, disproved this hypothesis. The children were very verbal with language development which demonstrated ability in all seven categories of language usage. The only deficit found was in the extent of their oral vocabulary. They had the *breadth* of language development, but lacked the *depth* of vocabulary to be considered completely proficient users of language.

The study of language process and function has led to a growing awareness that context plays a vital role in language learning and use. Children's language should not be studied in isolation, but in relation to the context in which it is used, and to the users' social and cultural backgrounds.[4] Children already know a great deal about language when they enter school. They know the linguistic structure and grammatical patterns of language. They know that language expresses meanings and is a way of sharing experiences and ideas. They know that language is functional and can be used to get things done, find out about things, make friends, complain or praise, and create imaginary worlds. As Halliday found,

> Children know what language is because they know what language does. The determining elements in the young child's experience are the successful demands on language that he himself has made, the particular needs that have been satisfied by language for him. . . . Language is, for the child, a rich and adaptable instrument for the realization of his intentions; there is hardly any limit to what he can do with it.[5]

Instruction should enable continued growth by encouraging and facilitating the use of the child's existing language skills and knowledge to build and expand those skills. Children acquire new knowledge only when they can relate it to ideas or language that makes sense in terms of their background. Whitehurst said, "People from poverty backgrounds are less likely to use language in which meaning adheres to the spoken or written word itself and more likely to use language that is adjusted to and depends on a particular social context for meaning."[6] Teachers must be aware of this and view the variations as *differences* to be built upon and not as *deficiencies* to be remediated or corrected.

Halliday identified three interrelated facets to language development: learning language, learning through language, and learning about language.[7]

Learning language is the process of acquiring the meanings and functions of language and learning the symbols to represent those meanings and functions both in oral and in written form. *Learning through language* is the process of using the language system to construct pictures of the world. While developing these systems, children also *learn about language* itself as they become cognizant of language in all its forms and functions. All three processes take place together and reinforce each other, and they are generally subconscious. Language is a social process that is learned in meaningful communication with others.

King defined language learning as an interactive process.[8] The learning is greater when children and adults share a common environment, and when that environment fosters understanding and growth. Language is a personal part of who one is. Therefore, an attack on one's speech is an attack on the innermost self.

Lindfors found that some of the clearest demonstrations of children's knowledge of language structure were found in their informal talk, language play, questioning, and comprehension of others.[9] Informal talk on the playground, at lunch, in the classroom or with teachers and aides reveals which language skills are well developed and which should be extended. It can also exhibit the meanings a child has learned for particular words. Children often play with language and word forms. The word forms children create and use can demonstrate linguistic knowledge and understanding.

In learning, children rely on interaction with others who share their interests in new experiences. The quality of these experiences and the relationships with others determines the knowledge they gain and the language they use. Genishi found that in order for children to become competent language users, they require knowledge about sounds, meanings, syntax, knowledge of social and linguistic rules that enable them to speak and interact appropriately in different situations.[10] They also gain the ability to participate in society with appropriate and recognizable communication. All these elements are acquired within the context of the culture in which they live.

Conflict between the child's culture and the culture of the school is often the basis of difficulties many children experience when they enter school. Homelessness is a culture in and of itself. Regardless of race, ethnicity, religion, or previous status, when a person becomes homeless, it becomes necessary to learn how to act appropriately in the culture of homelessness. It is necessary to learn where to go for assistance, how to ask for that assistance in the "proper" manner, and how to maintain one's sense of self where no privacy exists. Children in this culture quickly learn when to speak and when to remain quiet, when to be seen and when to remain "invisible." These cultural structures, interaction patterns, environment and values determine the child's behavior.

The transition from home to school is difficult for many children, but is especially troublesome for those whose experiences are least like those offered and valued by the school. Too often children are expected to fit into the curriculum of the school with very little attention to, or appreciation of, what they already know and can do. Hartle-Schutte says,

> [C]hildren from all socio-economic levels, races, and cultures within our nation become literate. What should be surprising is that so many reportedly do not become literate. Why, when virtually everyone achieves oral language ability, do we have large numbers of children and adults labeled illiterate? Why, at least according to traditional measures of success, are minority students less likely to be considered successful?[11]

We know that large differences in all aspects of language development can cause difficulties for children when they come to school. These differences include but are not limited to: how conversation participants relate to one another, interaction patterns, environment and values of the home, and how these aspects fail to match those of the school. Teachers must actively restructure the school curriculum so that the knowledge and experiences that each child brings to school are valued and built upon.

Joan Tough studied children's language at home and after school entry and claimed that most children were able to use language for maintaining status, directing actions, and talking about things in the present. They differed in their ability to recall relevant past experiences, make associations, analyze events, anticipate and predict, collaborate and sequence, and project into the future.[12] These latter uses of language tend to be the type children need for success in school. Children are expected to relate to the experiences of other children, the teacher, and the instructional materials. Their success is dependent on the ability to sequence events and make predictions. When there is a mismatch between the language abilities of the student, the requirements of the curriculum, and/or the expectations of the teacher, the student may be viewed as deficient and incapable of success.

Structural aspects of language such as dialectical differences represent only the surface of cultural variation. Less well known but perhaps more deep-seated differences exist in the rules which govern our interactions with each other—the system of social use. Just as children learn the forms of language in the context of their home communities, they learn how to use language with adults and peers in the same context. Misunderstandings between teacher and students may occur when patterns for group interaction differ. Wolfgang reported that misunderstandings between cultures may result from the use of nonverbal cues, facial expressions or gestures, and body language or positioning in relationship with others.[13] Cultural clashes can result when children do not engage in talk with adults of mainstream culture, or when they use inappropriate language or talk at what may be considered as the wrong time.

Syntactic forms vary among cultures. Teachers may be familiar with such forms, but they may not realize that such expressions follow rules appropriate to the speaker's cultural background. It would be well to remember what Hymes stated regarding these forms: "The vernacular speech of every society or social group, when studied, has been found to be based on complex, profound structures."[14]

King found that the context of learning is crucial.[15] The total learning situation has a powerful influence on whatever talk or writing occurs in the classroom. When children spend hour after hour in isolated tasks working on ditto sheets or filling in blanks in workbooks, they have little opportunity to talk or write for real purposes or to use language as it is used in the real world. The language context, the environment, and the climate of the classroom and school are, therefore, important factors that influence how children will use language. Context includes other people, expectations of communication, the backgrounds of both speakers and listeners, and the physical surroundings in which the interactions take place.

Kiefer and DeStefano observed that teachers are confronted with a variety of cultural differences as they use language to teach about language.[16] Often, the task of educating disintegrates into a struggle to impose "correct" or mainstream forms upon children who may be confused by and uncomfortable with such forms. Clay pointed out some difficulties with teachers helping children develop language proficiency. One difficulty is the bias that arises from the teacher's personal experience that may be limited to children of certain locations, class, or ability, and which affects that teacher's judgment. The second difficulty is the bias that comes from belief systems.[17] Teachers cannot teach without believing in the value of what they do. They are constantly confronted with choices regarding curriculum, materials, activities, questions. Such issues are decided by the educational values and goals held by the teacher. However, the teacher's values and goals may not match the values and goals of the culture of the students.

In a study of first graders, Pinnell found two elements were usually present as children actively engaged in functional use of language. The first element is that students encounter real problems they want to solve. The second element is that students work and talk about the problems.[18] Rather than seeing talk as distracting, the teachers view it as valuable and structured activities and the environment to take maximum advantage of the way children learn by giving them many opportunities to talk. The key to success is a teacher who is aware of the importance of fostering the use of language and who is a good observer. Talk facilitates learning as it helps children refine and organize their concepts.

Although Whitehurst asserts that children from low-income families have depressed levels of linguistic skills,[19] many studies have shown that minority children do become literate.[20] Having a single parent, limited income, severe social problems within the home, a first language other than English or a lower status dialect does not prevent literacy development. Thus, the classroom and the school must be thought of as a learning context in which everything helps teach the child. Evidence shows that, in the family environment, children learn from everything around them, even though very little direct instruction takes place.[21] Hasan makes the point that it is the relevant factors in the environment that influence the language used.[22] A serious problem in extending language and literacy in schools arises from the fact that so much of the content has been decontextualized. Reading, writing, and content areas have been removed from the real world of experience. Purpose and function may not be readily evident in much that goes on in the classroom. However, there are school contexts in which teachers acknowledge and use the contribution each child brings to his or her own learning. Within the school curriculum there must be room for children to follow their own interests and learn to take responsibility for learning. The teachers' role is powerful for they decide the way time and space are organized; how children go about learning; to what extent work is done collaboratively; when, what, and how reading or writing are done and the time spent doing it. In responding to students' work, they indicate values. They influence students' ideas by good stories, rich experiences, and talk and interaction. As teachers work with students, observing them carefully, they can make judgments about their understanding, their grasp of principles, their use of skills. By observing language use in the classroom, they can make assessments of individual development, competence and language skills.

In their longitudinal study, Hart and Risley found that economic advantage or disadvantage plays the most significant role in the language and vocabulary development of children.[23] They found that children living in poverty, children born into middle-class families, and children with professional parents all have the same kinds of everyday language experiences. They all hear talk about persons, things, relationships, actions, feelings, and about past and future events. They all participate in interactions in which they are prompted, responded to, prohibited, or affirmed. However, children in more economically privileged homes hear the positive interactions more often and the negative ones less often than children living in poverty. The differences between the families documented in this study were not in the *kinds* of experiences they provided their children but in the *amounts* of those experiences. The basic finding is that children who learn fewer words in their first three years also have fewer experiences with words in interactions with others, and they are also children growing up in less economically advantaged homes.

The data gathered during the 100 hours of classroom, playground, lunchroom and field trip observations were analyzed and conclusions and insights were examined to develop an effective description of the data. Since the sample was an ever-changing population and was composed of children of many ages and abilities, it was impossible to directly compare language usage among the children. It was possible, however, to observe patterns of language usage. Therefore, the categories of language usage developed by Halliday[24] with definitions formulated by Pinnell[25] were the most appropriate method for analysis.

Instrumental Language

Instrumental Language is "what we use to get what we want, to satisfy needs or desires."[26] One of the most frequently heard phrases was, "That's mine." Establishing ownership of supplies, personal belongings, and territory was extremely important. When one has little, it is vital to retain that small amount. Sharing of items was very difficult for many children and virtually impossible for a few of them. This problem was solved when the teacher simply made sure that no sharing was necessary by providing each child with his/her own paper, pencils, markers, and chair and table space.

Because of the shortage of space in shelters, it is much easier for a single man to get a bed than for a mother with one or more children. Therefore, the children have learned to become "invisible" when their mother is trying to get assistance and/or a bed for the night. They are very quiet, often hiding behind their mother while she speaks with shelter personnel. However, in other settings, the children are very verbal. They have mastered the boundaries and unspoken "rules" of the culture extremely well.

The homeless culture teaches that one must be polite in order to be given what one needs to survive, such as food and shelter. The children have learned this lesson well and are very polite when asking for permission to leave the room, use the teacher's supplies, obtain second servings of refreshments, and so forth. However, the children were very outspoken and competitive in seeking attention for actions and help with assignments. The culture also teaches this as the homeless must get "noticed" as individuals in order to be picked up for day labor jobs or individual assistance. As Pinnell notes, it is very important to be able to use instrumental language appropriately and effectively.[27]

Regulatory Language

Regulatory Language is used to control the behavior of others. This may include giving orders or manipulating and controlling others. Observation revealed a great deal of order-giving to control the immediate situation. Such things as, "Be quiet," "Stop that," and "Wait a minute" were frequently heard as the children worked and played. Cooperative group work was very difficult for these children because of the territorialism observed. Children ordered others to leave their belongings alone or to do their own work. As Pinnel points out, "Positive regulatory language is one of the 'life skills' that every parent, shop owner, foreman, or administrator must know."[28] It is essential for success in life.

Interactional Language

Interactional Language is used "to establish and define social relationships. It may include negotiation, encouragement, expressions of friendships, and the kind of 'maintenance' language all of us use in group situations."[29] Establishment of leadership was important. Several children emerged as natural leaders of the group and their orders were followed. While doing a worksheet, the following conversation with two second graders and the teacher was heard:

Jesse: "You have to color each little space a different color because
  each state has a different color."
Michael: "Okay, I'll make it green."

Teacher: "What are you doing, Michael?"
Michael: "He told me to color it green because he says it has rules for
         each state color."

Michael had interpreted Jesse's direction as an order with rules for the task at hand because Jesse was a leader, even when his leadership proved to be in a direction unacceptable to the teacher. He was a powerful influence on other children and conveyed his power both verbally and physically. Pinnell states that those who are effective in building interpersonal relationships are more likely to succeed.[30] Therefore, children must develop an awareness of the uses of language in connecting with other people, working in cooperation with them, and enjoying their company. Jesse built relationships based on his strength as a persuasive leader. However, he did not work well with others unless he was in that leadership role and the others were cooperating with him. He did not seem to enjoy companionship as much as he enjoyed his sense of power. This often caused a great deal of conflict in the classroom.

Personal Language

Personal Language is used to "express individuality and personality. Strong feelings and opinions are part of personal language."[31] The children enjoyed sharing stories about their families, their travels, and their plans. During a lunchtime discussion of what various children wanted to be when they grew up, Angel, a first grader, said, "When I grow up I'm not gonna be nothin'. I'm gonna set on my ass." When asked what he had said, he replied, "I'm gonna set on my chair." Several of the older children had chided Angel for his use of "a bad word." However, it was later learned that Angel had no other word in his vocabulary to name that part of his body. In his family, "ass" is the word that is used, and it clearly expressed what Angel intended.

Double negatives were used almost consistently in speech. "I ain't not gonna do it" or "I don't know nothin'" were common phrases around the classroom. Again, however, the intention of the speaker is very clear.

Pinnell says, "[I]t is through personal language that children relate their own lives to the subject matter being taught, establish their own identities, build self esteem and confidence."[32] These qualities were strongest in the children who could best express themselves both in and out of the classroom. Most of the children were very open. However, those most troubled, like Jesse and Eva, were very careful to maintain a distance in their relationships with the other children and the adults in the classroom. Distancing oneself can be a form of self-protection from being hurt emotionally. If one does not get close and learn to care about someone else, then one cannot be hurt when others leave or fail to respond as desired.

Imaginative Language

Imaginative Language is used "to create a world of one's own, to express fantasy through dramatic play, drama, poetry or stories."[33] The children exhibited a great deal of creativity, originality and imagination. They made up jump rope rhymes, songs, knock-knock jokes, and stories. The creative writing activities generated extensive works which the children acted out for one another. Making up knock-knock jokes occupied two whole hours on the playground and produced such jokes as the following which was made up by Josie: "Knock, knock." "Who's there?" "Prince." "Prince who?" "Prince S!" The children enjoyed playing with language as will be described more fully in Chapter 6.

Heuristic Language

Heuristic Language is used "to explore the environment, to investigate, to acquire knowledge and understanding."[34] The children asked many questions about this researcher: where I lived, what I did when I was not at the shelter, and about my family. On several occasions, a child asked a question in which he/she used an *incorrect* word, but one that conveyed the intended message very clearly. During a lunchtime conversation, a van with video equipment parked outside the window. Lorraine, a third grader, turned to me and asked, "Is he going to camera us?" In using the word "camera" as a verb, Lorraine had followed the rules of Standard English which allow nouns to become verbs in certain instances. She happened to use the incorrect noun, "camera," instead of the correct one, "film." Her language usage, however, followed the rules and clearly expressed her question. Pinnell defines this as language "for investigation, for wondering, for figuring things out. It is the language of inquiry and is one of the most important functions."[32] Clearly, Lorraine was using language to do these things.

Informative Language

Informative Language is used "to communicate information, to report facts or conclusions from facts. It is the language of school."[36] The children enjoyed sharing experiences and background knowledge. When studying about the Olympics, they knew what the games were, where they were to be held, and the names of many athletes who would be competing. When visiting the library on a field trip, they knew how to locate books they wanted to check out, they knew "proper behavior" in the library, and were able to explain these things to the adults who accompanied them on the trip. When studying about the ocean, they knew about ocean life and a great deal about the environment. Several children had lived in other parts of the country and were quick to share information regarding snow, salt water, deserts, lakes, and so forth. It was amazing to hear the variety of information, because it had been assumed that children in such extremely deprived circumstances would have deficient experiences and knowledge also. This was not the case. The children in the shelter knew many things that other children in other circumstances would know, and they also knew many things that other children in other circumstances would not know. They knew more about survival and had more coping skills than most middle class adults. They were much more "street wise" than any child should have to be. Most appeared eager to share what they knew with others almost to the point of being competitive.

Whitehurst found that "[c]hildren from low-income backgrounds develop language that is different in kind and degree from children in the general population."[37] However, this research found that, although there were differences in their language development, the children in the classroom at the homeless shelter had adequate language development. These differences should not be viewed as deficits. The children had the ability to express themselves in order to satisfy needs or desires; to control the behavior of others; to establish and define social relationships; to express individuality and personality; to create; to explore, investigate, acquire knowledge and understanding; and to communicate information. Although Standard English is not generally the language of the homeless culture, the children possessed adequate language for effective communication. Vocabulary development, though limited, was adequate for effective communication also. However, it too, did not match the Standard English used and required in school. Again, these were observed *differences*, not necessarily *deficits*.

Often a child's efforts to express him/herself were viewed as inappropriate or offensive when the problem was actually a lack of *appropriate* vocabulary as in Angel's use of the word "ass" during our lunchtime discussion.

Classrooms tend to be middle class environments with middle class teachers having middle class values and expectations. The problems arise when children from different cultures and different background experiences are required by the classroom culture, values and expectations to use middle class language with which they are not comfortable and which does not come *naturally*. It is the mismatch between the culture of the child and the culture of the school that is the source of the conflict and misunderstanding. This mismatch causes children, especially those from extreme poverty, to be labeled *deficient* or *disabled* when they do not perform according to the expectations of the school. The children are not deficient or disabled. They come to school with a wealth of background experiences which could be used as a basis for further learning and growth. Their experiences must be accepted as legitimate and used as that foundation.

Schools are obligated to extend the opportunities for children to use language to learn. Pinnell and Matlin found that the key to positive change in language education was increasing the professional knowledge and practical skills of teachers.[38] Teachers must recognize that children are active learners who will increase their understanding by using language to investigate and construct meaning. This process is only possible through interaction with others. "Teachers who see language instruction as helping children develop a whole range of potential ways for using language have many opportunities for doing so."[39] Teachers must build upon activities that allow students to explore language and participate in collaborative learning. As the children "focus on something interesting and enjoyable, they constantly practice a range of language functions."[40]

Accommodating the language structures with which students are familiar will enhance language usages so students can communicate more comfortably. It is important to remember that children are being prepared to live in a multicultural world and they will have to function efficiently in a variety of situations. Therefore, as Tough points out,

> The most important help that we can give to young children in school is likely to be through those experiences that foster the potential they have for using language as a means of thinking and communicating; in this way those children who are at a disadvantage when they come to school might develop new ways of interpreting their experiences and new meaning for their time in school.[41]

"The teacher's task is twofold: to provide learning situations where a variety of levels of informative language can be used and to communicate high value for interpreting and speculating."[42] The key to effective teaching is building on what students have already learned and the best way to discover this is to listen and watch closely as children use language in different settings and circumstances. As patterns of use emerge, teachers must reflect on them, compare them to past observations and knowledge of language development, and determine the competence and skill with language students possess.[43] The literacy experiences in the schools must mirror the authentic literacy functions, needs, and uses of the surrounding communities. Assessment techniques that look at what students *do* in the process of learning should be the focus of evaluation. This will provide more accurate information for designing instruction and helping students realize the purposes for learning.

Learners of every socio-economic and cultural group have the potential to be successful.[44] "If schools can only meet the needs of children who have had the 'school-valued' experiences, then the schools have failed."[45] Learning experiences must build upon what the children already know and prepare them for the demands of the *real* world. "Only then can we hope to achieve 'literacy and justice for all'."[46]

Notes

1.   Rubin, D. (2000). *Teaching elementary language arts: A balanced approach* (6th Ed.). Boston, MA: Allyn & Bacon, xxv.

2.   Halliday, M.A.K. (1973). The functional basis of language. In Bernstein (Ed.), *Class, codes, and control, volume . Applied studies toward a sociology of language.* Boston, MA: Routledge & Kegan Paul, 343-366.

Halliday, M.A.K. (1975). *Learning how to mean: Explorations in the development of language.* London, England: Edward Arnold Ltd.

3.   Goodman, K. (1996). Language development: Issues, insights, and implementation. In Power & Hubbard (Eds.), *Language development, A reader for teachers.* Englewood Cliffs, NJ: Prentice-Hall, Inc., 81.

4.   Jaggar, A. & Smith-Burke, M.T. (Eds.) (1985). *Observing the language learner.* Newark DE: International Reading Association and Urbana, IL: National Council of Teachers of English.

5.   Halliday, M.A.K. (1982). Relevant models of language. In B. Wade (Ed.), *Language perspectives*. London, England: Heinemann Educational Books, 40.

6.   Whitehurst, G.J. (1997). Language processes in context: Language learning in children reared in poverty. In Adamson & Romski (Eds.), *Communication and language acquisition: Discoveries from atypical development*. Baltimore, MD: Paul H. Brookes Publishing Co., 238.

7.   Halliday, M.A.K. (1980). Three aspects of children's language development: Learning language, learning through language, learning about language. In Goodman, Haussler, & Strickland (Eds*)*, *Oral and written language development research: Impact on the schools*. Urbana, IL: National Council of Teachers of English, 7-19.

8.   King, M.L. (1985). Language and language learning for child watchers. In Jaggar & Smith-Burke (Eds.), *Observing the language learner*. Newark, DE: International Reading Association and Urbana, IL: National Council of Teachers of English, 19-38.

9.   Lindfors, J.W. (1985). Understanding the development of language structure. In Jaggar & Smith-Burke (Eds.), *Observing the language learner*. Newark, DE: International Reading Association and Urbana, IL: National Council of Teachers of English, 41-56.

10.   Genishi, C. (1985). Observing communicative performance in young children. In Jaggar & Smith-Burke (Eds.), *Observing the language learner*. Newark, DE: International Reading Association and Urbana, IL: National Council of Teachers of English, 131-142.

11.   Hartle-Schutte, D. (1993). Literacy development in Navajo homes: Does it lead to success in school?. *Language Arts,* 70(8), 652.

12.   Tough, J. (1977). *The development of meaning: A study of children's use of language*. London, England: Allen & Unwin.

13.   Wolfgang, A. (1977). The silent language in the multicultural classroom. *Theory into practice, 16* (June), 145-157.

14.   Hymes, D. (1972). Introduction. In Cazden, John & Hymes (Eds.), *Functions of language in the classroom*. New York, NY: Teachers College Press, xx.

15.   King, M.L.

16.   Kiefer, B.Z. & DeStefano, J.S. (1985). Cultures together in the classroom: "What you sayin?." In Jaggar & Smith-Burke (Eds.), *Observing the language learner*. Newark, DE: International Reading Association and Urbana, IL: National Council of Teachers of English, 159-172.

17.   Clay, M.M. (1989). Involving teachers in classroom research. In Pinnell & Matlin (Eds.), *Teachers and research, language learning in the classroom*. Newark, DE: International Reading Association, 29-46.

18.   Pinnell, G.S. (1996). Ways to look at the functions of children's language. In Power & Hubbard (Eds.), *Language development, A reader for teachers*. Englewood Cliffs, NJ: Prentice-Hall, Inc., 146-154.

19.   Whitehurst, G.J.

20.   Goodman, K. & Goodman, Y. (1978). *Reading of American children whose language is a stable rural dialect of English or language other than English* (Final report, Project NIE-C-00-3-0087). Washington, DC: U.S. Department of Health, Education, and Welfare, National Institute of Education.

Harste, J., Woodward, V., & Burke, C. (1984). *Language stories and literacy lessons*. Portsmouth, NH: Heinemann.

Hartle-Schutte, D.

Heath, S.B. (1983). *The invisible culture: Communication in classroom and community on the warm springs Indian reservation*. New York, NY: Longman.

Taylor, D. & Dorsey-Gaines, C. (1988). *Growing up literate: Learning from inner-city families.* Portsmouth, NH: Heinemann.

   Teale, W.H. (1986). Home background and young children's literacy development. In Teale & Sulzby (Eds.), *Emergent literacy: Writing and reading.* Norwood, NJ: Ablex.

21.   Pinnell. (1996).
22.   Hasan, R. (1981). What's going on: A dynamic view of context in language. In Copeland (Ed.), *The seventh LACUS forum 1980.* Columbia, SC: Hernbeam Press, 106-121.
23.   Hart, B. & Risley T.R. (1995). *Meaningful differences in the everyday experiences of young American children.* Baltimore, MD: Paul H. Brookes Publishing Co.
24.   Halliday (1973) (1975).
25.   Pinnell. (1996).
26.   Ibid., 147.
27.   Ibid.
28.   Ibid., 147.
29.   Ibid., 147.
30.   Ibid.
31.   Ibid., 147.
32.   Ibid., 147.
33.   Ibid., 147.
34.   Ibid., 148.
35.   Ibid., 148.
36.   Ibid., 148.
37.   Whitehurst, 259
38.   Pinnell, G.S. & Matlin M.L. (Eds.) (1989). *Teachers and research, language learning in the classroom.* Newark, DE: International Reading Association.
39.   Pinnell, G.S. (2001). Language in primary classrooms. *Theory into practice,* 14(5). 320.
40.   Ibid., 320.
41.   Tough, 179.
42.   Pinnell (2001), 325.
43.   Jaggar, A. (1985). On observing the language learner: Introduction and overview. In Jaggar & Smith-Burke (Eds.), *Observing the language learner.* Newark, DE: International Reading Association and Urbana, IL: National Council of Teachers of English, 1-7.
44.   Rose, M. (1989). *Lives on the boundary.* New York, NY: Penguin Books.
45.   Hartle-Schutte, 652.
46.   Ibid., 653.

Chapter 6
Playing with Language

Children laugh an average of three hundred or more times a day;
adults laugh an average of five times a day; we have a lot of catching
up to do.
Heather King[1]

Freud believed that language play and creativity with words during early development are important parts of the whole process of learning language. He said,

> Before there is such a thing as a joke there is something that we may describe as "play" or "a jest". . . . It is not to be wondered at that these pleasurable effects encourage children in the pursuit of play and cause them to continue it without regard for the meaning of words or the coherence of sentences. Play with words and thoughts, motivated by certain pleasurable effects of economy, would thus be the first stage of jokes.[2]

Humor has been described as a social lubricant and laughter as the shortest distance between two people (attributed to Victor Borge, the famous humorist). Elementary school children are exposed to a repertoire of children's traditional wordplay. "Children love to make up and tell jokes and riddles; these examples of verbal humor are stories in miniature, offering an opportunity to practice language, conversation and social interaction skills during childhood."[3] Young children learn through imitating older students and then attempting to construct their own examples, usually on the playground.

Research shows that complex language skills like turn-taking and conversation control are developed and practiced in a language rich environment.[4] Humor may be undervalued for its part in developing language and social skills, because it appears to be a less than serious activity. However, research confirms that children are not just "playing." Playing with language offers opportunities for children to develop skills in a natural and enjoyable way. As they try various forms of wordplay, children are learning valuable information about how language works.[5] The linguist David Crystal states it is likely that "the greater our ability to play with language, the more we will reinforce the general development of metalinguistic skills, and—ultimately—the more advanced will be our command of language as a whole, in listening, reading, writing and spelling."[6]

Much of children's use of language, especially with peers, is humorous. It takes the form of jokes, riddles and silly rhymes as a natural part of conversations. This wordplay provides a structure in which children can experiment with words and sounds. The multiple meaning of some words and possible pronunciations in English can be used in all sorts of humor. Word knowledge and skills, such as the ability to switch the frame of reference, are required to understand the ambiguity found in wordplay. Laughter results when the ambiguity is resolved and when the play-on-words makes sense with the earlier information. Thus the appreciation and production of humor can assist in the development of more advanced language skills. Attempts at personal production of humor lead to greater understanding of the techniques, especially when there is feedback such as laughter from others. This acts as a scaffold for emerging and developing language skills.

Fowles and Glanz studied the ability and skill of children ages 5 to 9 to participate and comprehend verbal riddles. They said, "Children must . . . infer the relevant social and structural criteria for jokes and joke telling for themselves in order to distinguish jokes from non-jokes, to exhibit appropriate joke-telling behavior, and to determine what makes jokes funny."[7] Their findings show that the complexity of what makes jokes funny is the most complicated skill to develop; therefore, it is the last skill to develop in children. There are three factors involved in gaining competence with telling, participating in, and understanding riddles. First, the child must reach a cognitive developmental stage to be able to cope with two or more meanings of a word or phrase. This is reached at about seven years of age. Second, one must have cognitive and social familiarity with riddles and how to tell them. Third, there must be an ability to attend to the surface properties of language while moving one's thinking away from literal interpretation.

Learning to tell a joke is a complex task and the skill with which a joke can be executed increases with age and development. Outekhine said a joke is a narrative or anecdote.[8] He believes that specific narrative competence with language is required to remember and retell a joke. Berstein summarized the elements that must be recognized in a joke: understanding multiple meanings of words, metaphors and idioms; detecting ambiguity; perceiving incongruity; and appreciating the unexpected sudden shift of perspective.[9] The understanding of these elements increases with age and linguistic development.

Playing and being creative with words is an important part of the whole process of learning language. Over time, with practice, language skills mature, developing from the casual form of the school playground to the more regular structure of the classroom.

The knock–knock joke is probably the best known form of the pun/riddle and is a time-honored, structured exercise which follows specific structure for initiation, turn-taking, and punchline for the joke to "work." There are rules that must be followed for a knock-knock joke to be successful. It cannot work without both participants knowing something about this structure. The creation and telling of knock-knock jokes have been studied because they provide valuable insight into how children develop language skills.

One day on the shelter playground, during physical education/recess time, the children began to spontaneously share knock-knock jokes. All of the children wanted to participate in the activity and each in turn tried to construct his/her own joke. Some worked very well, just as the traditional knock–knock joke should. However, many younger children were not able to complete the play-on-words successfully. This can be seen in the examples of the knock-knock jokes told by the children.

Kindergarten and First Graders

Student: Knock, knock.
Teacher: Who's there?
Student: Basketball.
Teacher: Basketball who?
Student: I'm a basketball. So are you.

Student: Knock, knock.
Teacher: Who's there?
Student: Pig.
Teacher: Pig who.
Student: Didn't you just see you stepped on a black pig.

Student: Knock, knock.
Teacher: Who's there?
Student: Dug.
Teacher: Dug who?
Student: Didn't you see that hole I just dug.

Student: Knock, knock.
Teacher: Who's there?
Student: Dr. Davenport.
Teacher: Dr. Davenport who?
Student: Dr. Davenport that's who.

Crystal suggests that playing with words and understanding the syntax of riddles may help in acquiring skills with grammar.[10] Telling puns and engaging in nonsense talk promotes links with the development of syntax and word pronunciations. For the children at the shelter, nonsense was a way of exploring the very nature of language. They played with patterns of sounds and the rhythms of speech. They tried to make puns and plays-on-words similar to their older companions on the playground. They thoroughly enjoyed these jokes and laughed at the ones they and their classmates told. However, it is readily evident in the above examples that these younger children did not understand the construction patterns for the jokes which make the punchlines work in the traditional sense of a play-on-words.

Second Graders

Student: Knock, knock.
Teacher: Who's there?
Student: Donna.
Teacher: Donna who?
Student: Donna you have a ball in your head.

Student: Knock, knock.
Teacher: Who's there?
Student: Joe.
Teacher: Joe who?
Student: Joseph.

Student: Knock, knock.
Teacher: Who's there?
Student: Jellybean.
Teacher: Jellybean who?
Student: A jellybean bean
          (been) by you.

Student: Knock, knock.
Teacher: Who's there?
Student: Pig
Teacher: Pig who?
Student: Pig-a-dory.

Student: Knock, knock.
Teacher: Who's there?
Student: Goosebumps.
Teacher: Goosebumps who?
Student: Haven't you had the
          goosebumps look?

Wordplay is instrumental in acquiring more mature speech forms. Children learn to play with the sounds of words and letters from the time they begin to babble. This "play" leads to the development of more mature communication skills.[11] Children at this age were beginning to master the language patterns found in knock-knock jokes. The ones made by this group of children show the ability to more closely approximate the true construction pattern of the joke. In particular, the one about the jellybean and the one about Joe contain very close approximations to the "imperfect" pun—constructions in which one similar-sounding word or phrase is humorously substituted for another. They also were able to make the type of play-on-words required for standard knock-knock jokes.

Third Graders

Student: Knock, knock.
Teacher: Who's there?
Student: Tummy.
Teacher: Tummy who?
Student: Tummy Ache.

Student: Knock, knock.
Teacher: Who's there?
Student: Apple.
Teacher: Apple who?
Student: Applesauce.

Student: Knock, knock.
Teacher: Who' there?
Student: Bug.
Teacher: Bug who?
Student: Bugs Bunny.

Student: Knock, knock.
Teacher: Who's there?
Student: Pea.
Teacher: Pea who?
Student: Pee Wee.

Student: Knock, knock.
Teacher: Who's there?
Student: Liz.
Teacher: Liz who?
Student: Lizard

Student: Knock, knock.
Teacher: Who's there?
Student: Feeling.
Teacher: Feeling who?
Student: Feeling well.

Student: Knock, knock.
Teacher: Who's there?
Student: Spider.
Teacher: Spider who?
Student: Spider web

Student: Knock, knock.
Teacher: Who's there?
Student: Soft
Teacher: Soft who?
Student: Softball.

As can be seen in these examples, the children at this age were beginning to get the idea of the knock-knock joke as a play-on-words. In this stage of development, verbal skills were explored in wordplay and jokes. In these middle elementary years, the children's repertoire for playing with language had grown in diversity, in the competence with which it was executed, and in the complexity of patterns of sound, sense and nonsense. Although not too complicated in structure, these jokes do work with the punchline giving an extension of the word at the beginning of the joke. All the children found each of these jokes enjoyable and very funny, and each child continued to try to add to our collection.

Fourth and Fifth Graders

Student: Knock, knock.
Teacher: Who's there?
Student: Boo.
Teacher: Boo who?
Student: Why you crying?

Student: Yeah. Knock, knock.
Teacher: Who's there?
Student: Shake.
Teacher: Shake who?
Student: Shake your bootie.

Student: Knock. Knock.
Teacher: Who's there.
Student: Crocodile
Teacher: Crocodile who?
Student: Crocodile Dundee that's
        who.

Student: Knock, knock.
Teacher: Who's there?
Student: Prince.
Teacher: Prince who?
Student: Princess

Student: I'll tell you a long one. Knock, knock.
Teacher: Who's there?
Student: Banana.
Teacher: Banana who?
Student: Knock, knock.
Teacher: Who's there?
Student: Banana.
Teacher: Banana who?
Student: Knock, knock.
Teacher: Who's there?
Student: Banana.
Teacher: Banana who?
Student: Knock, knock.

Teacher: Who's there?
Student: Orange.
Teacher: Orange who?
Student: Orange (aren't) you glad I didn't say
         banana?

These knock-knock jokes by the older children show more advanced de-
velpment of the ability to construct the "imperfect" pun. "The punning technique
of using a word once as a whole and then in parts is a form these children . . . are
able to appreciate."[12] The children delighted in the incongruity of words and
phrases with "twisted" meanings. As the oldest students on the playground, they
set the tone and pattern for the younger ones to try to imitate.

Early research showed that comprehension of humor improves with age and
the development of cognitive skills.[13] The growth in understanding of how the
knock-knock joke is constructed and how the punchline works is very well illustrated in the following examples. The older students began making jokes around
the word "corn" and the others tried to follow the pattern.

A fifth grader told this version of the "corn" joke:

Student: Knock, knock.
Teacher: Who's there?
Student: Acorn.
Teacher: Acorn who?
Student: A corn on your toe hurts.

A third grader followed with this version:

Student: Knock, knock.
Teacher: Who's there?
Student: Corn.
Teacher: Corn who?
Student: Corn-on-the-cob.

A second grader gave this version:

Student: Miss, I know one. Knock, knock.
Teacher: Who's there?
Student: Corn.
Teacher: Corn who?
Student: Your teeth are corn.

A first grader then tried this nonsensical rhyme:

Student: Knock, knock.

Teacher: Who's there?
Student: Corn.
Teacher: Corn who?
Student: Corn on your horn.

And finally, a kindergarten student attempted to give her version but was unable to complete the punchline:

Student: Knock, knock
Teacher: Who's there?
Student: Corn.
Teacher: Corn who?
Student: Corn..um....What was I gonna say?

To understand and appreciate verbal humor, children must go beyond the literal interpretation of the statement and recognize what is not overtly stated. They must pay attention to the structure of words and sentences and have some knowledge of the wider world. These abilities are acquired and developed with age, experience and practice. The flawed knock-knock jokes represent stages in a developmental progression. The youngest children were at the beginning stage in which they had mastered the generic form of the routine but did not recognize the entirety of it or understand the play-on-words in the standard joke. They tried to complete the joke by making up their own punchline which generally did not really complete the play-on-words. The older the child, the closer he/she could come to the true form of the knock-knock joke. The flawed renditions, together with the good ones, exemplify stages in the acquisition of competence. They are indicators of the range of cognitive and communicative skills, not merely *mistakes* to be disqualified in research data.

Sometimes the jokes were purely nonsensical, but everyone enjoyed them and joined in uproarious laughter to show appreciation.

Student: Knock, knock.
Teacher: Who's there?
Student: Dwayne.
Teacher: Dwayne who?
Student: Dwayne the Wayne
             I dropped my ducky.

Student: Knock, knock.
Teacher: Who's there?
Student: Hi.
Teacher: Hi who?
Student: Hi. Bye.

Student: Knock, knock.

Teacher: Who's there?
Student: Water.
Teacher: Water who?
Student: There's a bunch of water
        coming down on you.

Student: Knock, knock.
Teacher: Who's there?
Student: Water buffalo.
Teacher: Water buffalo who?
Student: You're standing on a water buffalo.
Teacher: You're silly.
Student: I know I am.

Sometimes the punchline came in the form of a spontaneous nonsensical rhyme:

Student: Knock, knock.
Teacher: Who's there?
Student: Tom.
Teacher: Tom who?
Student: Tom's been to Vietnam.

Student: Knock, knock.
Teacher: Who's there?
Student: Key.
Teacher: Key who?
Student: There's a key inside of
        your knee.

Student: Knock, knock.
Teacher: Who's there?
Student: Rock.
Teacher: Rock who?
Student: I pulled a rock out of my sock.

Learning to participate in social exchange is more than a matter of learning correct usage. It implies that the user understands the procedures and expectations of such exchanges. Conversations are a form of temporary partnership which is governed by social conventions. Certainly the exchange of knock-knock jokes has a pattern and expectations for how it will progress and how it will end. To a certain extent, a knock-knock joke follows the typical classroom question/answer format that teachers use to assess students' understanding of the instruction, reading material, and/or discussion. It is proposed that successful communication, often through humorous exchanges and playing with language, is an essential tool for gaining maturity and independence. It allows individuals to develop self-image and personal identity. "This is enculturation within the peer group."[14] Research has suggested that interactive communication, independence and personal identity are closely intertwined.[15] The importance of playing with language cannot be overemphasized. McGhee has found that people often use humorous language to ease the tension or stress of difficult situations.[16] In her research of children's uses of humor, Martha Wolfenstein proposed that during difficult times, children use humor in many positive ways. Humor can change a painful event into a more enjoyable one, turn the powerful and overbearing into the ridiculous, reveal adult flaws, and make light of failures.[17]

In a review of literature on humor and stress, Lefcourt and Thomas concluded that there is evidence to encourage the belief that humor can have positive effects in alleviating distress.[18] McGhee even found that humor may allow the expression of hostility in a socially acceptable manner and can also ease tense interactions with other people.

> Given the numerous positive social functions associated with the effective initiation of humor, and the positive relationship with measures of social competence, the development of heightened skills at initiating humor clearly makes a significant contribution to children's social development.[19]

For the homeless children these are vital functions of the use of humor in interactions and communications.

Spector found using humor had great possibilities for helping students improve turn-taking behavior, organize and present verbal material in proper sequence, and act appropriately as a listener and a speaker.[20] Certainly these are behaviors teachers want their students to develop and demonstrate. Although we may not hear much wordplay in classrooms because teachers think of this as a very non-serious activity, we cannot ignore the many spontaneously and/or ritually exchanged examples of humorous and playful language among children on the playgrounds, in hallways, and in lunchrooms. Wordplay activities can be valuable teaching/learning tools and should be included in education programs.[21] Humor and language play can be powerful and important teaching/learning tools in any classroom.

Teachers must guard against the tendency to suppress children's delight in absurdity. They should not always insist on literal or exact renditions of things. Sometimes stopping such play with language is justified because of the nature of the situation. However, teachers should encourage such explorations when it is appropriate. They can do so by encouraging playing with language and appreciating children's inventions. Teachers can even participate in this delightful adventure of wordplay and nonsense themselves.[22] As Crystal said, "Everyone plays with language or responds to language play. Some take mild pleasure from it; others are totally obsessed by it; but no one can avoid it." [23]

Notes

1. King, H. (1994). *Crib Notes*. New York, NY: Avon Books. Retrieved 12/13/06 from http://education.yahoo.com/reference/quotations/quote/42815.

2. Freud, S. (1991). *Jokes and their relation to the unconscious.* London, England: Penguin Library. Original publication,1905. 177-178.

3. O'Mara, D. (2004). Providing access to verbal humor play for children with se-

vere communication impairment. unpublished doctoral thesis. Applied Computing
Division,   University   of   Dundee,   Scotland.   Retrieved   10/8/2004   from
http://www.computing.dundee.ac.uk/staff/domara/home.asp, i.
    4.   Waller, A.; O'Mara, D.; Tait, L.; Hood, H.; Booth, L.; & Brophy-Arnott, B.
(2001). Using written stories to support the use of narrative in conversational interaction:
An AAC Case Study. *Augmentative and alternative communication*, 17, 221-232.
    5.   Geller, L.G. (1985). *Wordplay and language learning for children*. Urbana, IL:
National Council of Teachers of English.
    6.   Crystal, D. (1998). *Language play*. London, England: Penguin Books, 181.
    7.   Fowles, B. & Glanz, M.E. (1976). Competence and talent in verbal riddle com-
prehension. *Journal of child language*, 4, 437.
    8.   Outekhine, I. (1998). *Children's jokes: A developmental approach*. Paper pre-
sented at Imatra, Semiotic Symposium. St. Petersburg, Russia.
    9.   Bernstein, D.K. (1986). The development of humor: Implications for assess-
ment and intervention. *Topics in language disorders* (1), 47-58.
    10.   Crystal.
    11.   Ibid.
    12.   Geller, 79.
    13.   Fowles & Glanz
        McGhee, P. (1971). Development of the humor response: A review of the lit-
erature. *Psychological bulletin*, 76, 328-348.
        Shultz, T.R. & Horibe, F. (1974). Development of the appreciation of verbal
jokes. *Developmental psychology*, 10, 13-20.
    14.   Bauman, R. (1982). Ethnography or children's folklore. In Gilmore & Glat-
thorn (Eds.), *Children in and out of school, ethnography and education*. Washington,
D.C.: Center for Applied Linguistics, 178.
    15.   Waller, A. (1992). *Providing narratives in an augmentative communication
system*. Unpublished doctoral thesis. Applied computing division, University of Dundee,
Scotland.
        Waller, A.; O'Mara, D.; Tait, L.; Hood, H.; Booth, L.; & Brophy-Arnott, B.
        O'Mara, D.; Waller, A.; Tait, L.; Hood, H.; Booth, L.; & Brophy-Arnott, B. (2000).
Developing personal identity through story telling. *IEE colloquium on speech and lan-
guage processing for disabled and elderly people*. ISBN 0963-3308.
    16.   McGhee, P. (1996). *Health, healing and the amuse system*. Dubuque, IA: Ken-
dall Hunt Publishing Co.
    17.   Wolfentein, M. (1978). *Children's humor*. South Bend IN: Indiana University
Press.
    18.   Lefcourt, H.M. & Thomas, S. (1998). Humor and stress revisited. In Ruch
(Ed.), *The sense of humor: Explorations of a personality characteristic*. New York, NY:
Mouton de Gruyter, 179-202.
    19.   McGhee, P. (1989). The contribution of humor to children's social develop-
ment. *Journal of children in contemporary society*, 20, 131.
    20.   Spector, C.C. (1990). Linguistic humor comprehension of normal and language
impaired adolescents. *Journal of speech and hearing disorders*, 55, 533-541.
    21.   Geller.
    22.   Ibid.
    23.   Crystal, 1.

Chapter 7
Classrooms in the Projects

*At the beginning, the center, and the end of the educative process is
the child, whose proper development is the ideal.*
Dorothy Rubin[1]

The concentration of poverty among all school-aged children varies appreciably
according to the urbanism of school districts. In 1999, 24 percent of school-age
children lived in poverty if they were in school districts of large central metropolitan areas. Twenty percent of children lived in poverty in school districts of
midsize central metropolitan areas.[2] In San Antonio, some 30.7 percent of children live in high-poverty neighborhoods.[3] The site for this portion of the study
was an elementary school in the San Antonio Independent School District located in a subsidized housing project on the near southwest side of the city. In
order to qualify for residence in these apartments, income must be below the
poverty line and residents have to be receiving assistance such as welfare or
other government subsidies. The school is one of the oldest in the district with
almost 800 students.

Before the McKinney-Vento Act, which prohibited school or classroom
segregation of children because of living conditions,[4] the children from the San
Antonio homeless shelter were transferred from the one-room shelter classroom
to the school. One classroom in the school had been established for these children. So the children were still isolated from non-homeless children even in this
new setting. The teacher for this classroom was the same one who had taught
them in the shelter.

In 1994, the Texas Education Agency determined that this school, like
many others in the state, was not providing an acceptable level of quality education for its students. This judgment was based on student performance on the
standardized test used across the State of Texas. The school was given two years
to improve test scores. The school did improve student performance and had
been removed from the "unacceptable" list. However, to accomplish this improvement, the school instituted an extremely intensive program of training and
teaching for the test objectives. Students drilled and practiced on test objectives
daily, took practice tests weekly, and had limited time and experience with
teaching/learning that was not directly assessed by the state test.

Since the school is located within the subsidized housing project, the children are all of lower socio-economic status, with 75% of them coming from single parent homes. The demographics of the school reflect that of the surrounding area, 97% Hispanic, 2% Anglo, 1% African-American, with 100% of the students on free/reduced breakfast and lunch. In the classrooms where observations and data collection were done, the population was as follows:

GRADE	NUMBER	ETHNICITY	GENDER
K	15	100% Hispanic surname	10 boys, 5 girls
K	15	100% Hispanic surname	7 boys, 8 girls
1	17	14 Hispanic surname 3 Anglo surnames	9 boys, 8 girls
1	18	100% Hispanic surname	8 boys, 10 girls
2	15	100% Hispanic surname	6 boys, 9 girls
2	16	100% Hispanic surname	7 boys, 9 girls
3	21	100% Hispanic surname	9 boys, 12 girls
3	22	100% Hispanic surname	11 boys, 11 girls
4	18	100% Hispanic surname	10 boys, 8 girls
4	17	100% Hispanic surname	8 boys, 9 girls

The classroom for children from the homeless shelter had 6 students: Josie, Jesse, Angela and Eva, along with a first grade boy and a second grade girl. Josie was now in first grade, Jesse in third, Angela in fourth and Eva still in fifth grade having been held back. Before the observations were completed, Jesse was sent to the alternative school because of his extreme misbehavior and rebellious attitude.

The total population in classrooms used during observations was 180, 87 boys, 93 girls, 98 percent of whom had Hispanic surnames.

The data were gathered during 100 hours of classroom, playground, and lunchroom observations. The same categories of language usage developed by Halliday[5] with definitions formulated by Pinnell[6] were used for analysis of interactions, then comparisons were made between the interactions in the shelter classroom and interactions in the elementary school classrooms.

Children's knowledge about sounds, meanings, and syntax is *linguistic competence*. The knowledge of social and linguistic rules that enable people to speak and interact appropriately in different situations is *communicative competence*. What is observed in classrooms as children listen, speak, or write are aspects of their *communicative performance*. Pinnell says, "Children learn to talk within a network of social relationships in their homes. They are surrounded by talking people. They listen; they participate; and they acquire knowledge of language and its possible uses for communication."[7] Students' communicative performances in the elementary school classrooms were the object of this portion of the study.

Examples of *Instrumental Language* heard during observations in the elementary school classrooms:

"Explain me" (direct translation of a reflexive verb in Spanish)

Child in trouble, trying to explain situation to secretary:
    "Ms. Montez don't let me do it like that."

"He step me and I fell." (meaning, "He tripped me.")

Explaining a situation in the back of the classroom to the teacher:
    Child: "He's crying."
    Teacher: "Who's crying?"
    Child: "Alfonso because he didn't win."
    Teacher: "What's wrong, Alfonso? Why are you crying?"
    Alfonso: "I didn't won that's why."

It is evident in these exchanges that students are conveying a message that is important to them. They want action to be taken by another to rectify a situation of some sort. It is also evident that these students do not possess the Standard English phrasing and/or vocabulary that would make them appear as fluent speakers of English with the ability to express themselves well. This lack of English proficiency was much more evident in the school than it had been in the shelter classroom.

The uses of *Regulatory Language* fell into five categories: *Arguing, Gatekeeping, Rule Enforcement, Banter and Teasing,* and *Tattling*.

Arguing was observed primarily in grades three through five. Very little arguing was seen in kindergarten through second grade. Examples of Arguing Regulatory Language are:
    First 3rd grade boy: "Joe, did you think I didn't see it?"
    Second 3rd grade boy: "Potatohead? Shut up!"

Angelo and Luis arguing over a remark made by Angelo:
    Angelo: "Move, Louis, you're fat."
    Luis: "I'm not fat. Look at me. He's calling me fat. I'm not fat, I'm skinny, right?" (looking at Angelo) "I'm skinny, I'm not fat."

Angelo: "Yes you are. You kick my butt. You kick everybody's butt."

A fifth grade girl even argued with the teacher:
"Miss could I go sit over there?"
Teacher: "No."
Fifth grade girl: "Aye Chihuahua! You never let me do nothing. Can I go over there?"
Teacher: "No."
Fifth grade girl: "No fair!"

Third grade girls arguing in line:
First girl: "You cut the line."
Second girl: "I didn't cut you. I didn't cut you."

Gatekeeping was observed primarily in grades one and two. Examples of this type of Regulatory Language are:
"You're supposed to be in our group."
"Can I play?"
"No, we're gonna be in our center—just our group. We're just gonna play."

Girl to Stephanie: "You have to leave. Me and Chela are already here reading."

Rule Enforcement was observed in every grade level and in all locations—classrooms, cafeteria, and playground. Examples are as follows:
During a card game:
"You were dealer. You were passing them out. I go first because I had this one."
"He gots red."
"Man, you got a lot a red."
"Play the wild card cause you always tell us play the wild."
During a Scrabble game:
"I'll keep the score. No, no, there's lot's of letters for both of us. Put those right there for both of us. Don't just leave them like that. Don't, man, just behave!"
"Shhh! listen!"
In P.E. class, turning a jump rope:
"Make sure the knot is off."
"After 4 goes 1. We got to go that one."
In one class, a girl laid a paper on an object cut out by a boy. He said, "Wash out. You're stepping on it."
Girl commenting to a boy on his homework: "You leave a big space."
Vanessa to Leroy: "You write how much is this."

Banter and Teasing were primarily recorded in grades three and higher and were as follows:

During a Scrabble game:

"Can you give me a 'p' and I'll trade you for any letter."

"I would trade you but you'll win."

After a delay in game:

"I want to play."

"You're getting me nervous." (Big laughs)

Tattling was observed in every grade level and in all locations. Examples are as follows:

"Miss, she threw me the tongue!"

"Miss, I can't see. Look they're in the way!"

"I want to pick up the cards."

"Julia's getting the cards and she doesn't want to let me play."

"Miss, she told me I can't call out the cards. I'm gonna call out the cards. Can I call out the cards? Miss, look it! Miss, look it! This one, look it. Este, mira."

Regulatory Language occurred in all grade levels and in all locations—classrooms, cafeteria, playground and hallways. However, only Rule Enforcement and Tattling were totally universal. These are the two most directive forms of Regulatory Language used in an attempt to control others. Gatekeeping appeared primarily in grades one and two as attempts at controlling others, while Arguing and Banter and Teasing were observed at the upper elementary grades. It appears that some forms of Regulatory Language may be more sophisticated than others and require more experience and maturity to use.

Interactional Language is used to establish and define social relationships. It has been stated by Pinnell that "because those who are effective in building informal relationships are likely to succeed, children need to develop a comfortable awareness of their ability to use language to establish relationships with other people, to work cooperatively with them, and to enjoy their companionship."[8]

Examples of the *Interactional Language* observed in the classrooms are as follows:

"nino!" expressed when a "difficult" fraction was given to Maximo

"oh, que no!" when a fraction was illustrated and they were asked to say the fraction

Class was supportive of each other: "Good job, Maximo."

Polite responses to teacher: "No Ma'am." "Thank you." "Yes, Ma'am."

Polite responses to each other: "Thank you, Denise."

Teacher: Not every one is going to get a chance to come up today.

Marco: Oh, I want to take a chance.

When the assignment was given: "Aye, mama."
Conversation between two little girls and a boy named Juan:
>First girl: "Why is Juan crying? Who made Juan cry?"
>Second girl: "I think it was Julie."
>Juan: "No, it's not Julie. It's teacher."

Interaction between two children playing Bingo:
>First child: "Did you won me?"
>Second child: "Yes, this is my lucky, lucky card."

Conversation between a child and the researcher:
>Child: "I saw you over there?"
>Researcher: "Yes, in the hall when you were coming in?"
>Child: "You were looking at that thing (poster on hall wall) and at the book on your hand." (I was copying what parents had written of their dreams for their children.)

Conversation between a child and the researcher during lunchtime was overheard and interrupted by others joining in:
>Child: "I went to Sea World."
>Researcher: "Who did you go with?"
>Child: "My mom and my tia and my cousins."
>Researcher: "What was your favorite part?"
>Others: "The charks"
>Child: "I went to Lost Lagoon and there's these waves and you have to jump over them."

Conversation where Amelia explained her actions to a boy who had misunderstood her intentions:
>Boy: "Hey, you wrote on mine!"
>Amelia: "I know, I wrote it for you cause you're my friend."

In a conversation between a boy and girl in kindergarten regarding a game they had just played:
>Boy: "I never won, that's why I'm crying."
>Girl: "You can won next time."
>Boy: "I know, you can quit saying it."

The children in the Elementary School enjoyed talking to each other, to their teachers, and to the researcher. They openly shared information and often responded to each other in a polite and gracious manner. Even though some of their phrasing or terminology was incorrect, the use of Interactional Language certainly was well developed. The range was there, but the depth was lacking due to limited vocabulary development.

Personal Language is used to express individuality and personality. As Pinnell found, it is through the use of this type of language that children relate their own experiences to the curriculum.[9] They also use personal language to define their own personalities and identities and to build their own confidence. These qualities were strongest in the children who could best express themselves both in and out of the classroom.

Examples of *Personal Language* observed in classrooms were as follows:

Exchange between a fifth grade girl and the researcher regarding a necklace the researcher was wearing:

> Girl: "What is that—a shell?"
> Researcher: nod
> Girl: "Where did you get it?"
> Researcher: "Boston. Have you ever been to the beach?"
> Girl: "No. I been to Virginia Beach."
> Researcher: "Why?"
> Girl: "Cause, cause I just wanted to go there."
> Researcher: "Did you go by yourself?"
> Girl: "No, my dad"

In a second grade class, a girl arrived at 11:00 after a visit to the dentist. She modeled complete and elaborated sentences to explain her tardiness to the teacher and her experiences to her classmates.

During a discussion, a fourth grader told the class, "When we came from Mexico, my dad he got a rattlesnake with his hand. First he threw a rock to it, but it was already dead."

Alfredo liked to play at flirting. He quoted a song, "I'm gonna take it fast. Are you gonna take it serious?"

Several of the boys bragged on being the worst class in school:
"We're no. 1! We're no. 1!"
"Once we had 2 subs 'cause we're so bad"
"Did I behave bad?"

"Look, me and her are almost finished."

When talking about working together, one girl said to another, "Me and you, right?"

Commenting on why he couldn't do his work, a boy said, "I keep on forgotting."

Chela: "Look how much papers I did."

After running during P.E. class, a girl told the researcher, "If I sweat any more I'm going to faint."

With the exception of Regulatory Language, Personal Language usage was the most frequently observed and recorded. It would appear that this is one of the first categories of usage to develop and one of the primary ones used by individuals. Certainly the children at the elementary school used this form of language extensively and well.

Imaginative Language, used to create a world of one's own, to express fantasy through dramatic play, drama, poetry or stories, was the language that flourished in the kindergarten with its house corner, big blocks and toys. Unless it is fostered, it tends to disappear in later years. Its importance cannot be underestimated, especially considering how difficult some teachers find it to get students to write with imagination. Poetry, stories, and drama are all the result of active use of the imaginative function.

Examples of *Imaginative Language* usage were found primarily in the kindergarten classrooms and were as follows:

Playing with Legos and a balloon, one kindergarten boy said to another:
"I'm making Star Wars. Look this is how you make Star Wars."
Second boy: "Where you got the balloon from?"
First boy: "I made Star Wars—look it."
Second boy: "I could make something and then I could karate it."

While playing with blocks, two girls built houses:
"I'm making different things. Yours aren't gonna be like mine. I'm making different things like a princess castle. Let's be the princesses."

Jose: "This is my red sugar." (large domino with red spots)
Eli: "How come you didn't give me one. You got 2."
Jose: "Get your own. I got too much sugars."
Eli, holding up another domino: "I got my own sugars."

Examples found in the upper grades were as follows:

Discussing a presentation by a dental hygienist, a fourth grader said, "The rats get your teeth then they give you a dollar."

Play with language: "o la, e la, mo la, goo goo, ga, ga. Ace Bentura."

Play on words: "calculators—ca—ca—lators" (caca being the slang word of excrement)

Joke told by fifth graders
"Why do they cross the border by twos?"
"Because it says no trespassing."
"Get it? No tres (three) passing? Funny, huh?"

Exchange between the researcher and a fifth grade boy when told he should do his school work:

Boy: "Miss, I wanna flunk in 8th grade so I can work in McDonald's. I will take your order. Yes, ma'am, what will you have?"
Researcher: "A Big Mac, fries and a large shake."
Boy: "Yes, ma'am. Here you are." He held out his hands with an imaginary tray of food for the Researcher.

Heuristic Language is used to explore and acquire knowledge and figure things out. These are important functions of language for success in school.[10]

Examples of *Heuristic Language* were:

Student: "A fraction is like when you broke your arm or something, no?"

Teacher: "No, that's a fracture. This is a fraction."

Samantha could not recall the word for park.
"You know that place with the baseball fields and the swings and the big pool."

Student: "How do you call it when a man is bald head and they put a wig on it?"
Teacher: "Toupee."
Student: "How do you call it—a hair cutter?"
Teacher: " Barber."

"I don't get the last one." (when answering a teacher's question)
"Miss, I got a 88, right?"
"Miss, I didn't spell Lucas." (Translation: "I can't spell Lucas" or "Would you spell Lucas for me?")
"Who graded mines?"
"Where I go?" (2nd grader to parent in parking lot.)
"Can you lend me a paper?"
"What time do I be here?"
"What does observing mean?" (Question asked while reading a 5th grade science book)

A great deal of questioning and clarifying took place at all grade levels and in many locations. Most often the questions took a less than Standard English form, but nonetheless, were clearly understood and answered by others. When examined carefully, the forms of the questions were direct translations of the Spanish form.

Informative Language is used to communicate information, to report facts, or draw conclusions from facts. As Pinnell has said, "It is the language of school."[11] Teachers most frequently use it themselves and require it of children, but informative language is not only recall of facts. Helping children synthesize material and draw inferences and conclusions is also important.

Examples of *Informative Language* observed in the classrooms were as follows:

generating adjectives for *friends*

nice	excited	kind	lovely	not jealous
surprised	sweet	good	not mean	friendly
special	beautiful	happy	helpful	pretty
not gloomy	not sad	not lonely	sharing	funny

not angry   bright smile   good listener   pretty in their heart

After adjectives were generated by the children, they were asked to use them to describe someone in room while the rest of the class tried to guess who was being described.

"she's nicely" (used several times by one child and then modeled correctly by teacher each time)
"She has a pretty heart."
"you want to hug them" (teacher modeling huggable)
Other examples found in classrooms were as follows:
"A sheetah (cheetah) is the fastest animal, no?"

Teacher: "How can we check this subtraction problem?"
Student: "By plussing."
Teacher: "By adding, right."

A kindergartner returning to the classroom from the restroom, told his teacher, "Ms. Montez, the water is filling up at the toilet."

"I asked her sorry."

Student: "Miss, he don't have any."
Teacher: "He doesn't have any."

Student: "They don't got remainders."
Teacher: "They don't have remainders."

"I don't got no pockets."

Teacher: "She's crushed—that means she's really. . . ."
Child: "Sad."

Teacher: "What are some of our question words?"
Chela: "Choose, me."
Teacher: "Question word—when we're asking someone questions."
Chela: "Is, Why, How"
Michael: "What, Who, Can"
Amanda: "When, Are"
Michelle: "Do, Where"
Amelia: "Will, Do"

After a child said "Then":
Teacher: "Give me a question sentence starting with then."
Amanda: "Then will he come out and play?"

Teacher: "Take off then and start with the next word."
Amanda: "Will he come out and play?"
Teacher: "So what is the question word?"
Amanda: "Then—no,will."

The first day the researcher was introduced and they were told she was looking at how third graders acted. One third grader responded, "But we're only one—she won't see all of 3rd grade if she only sees us."

During a reading lesson in fourth grade:
"Miss, I knew she looked like someone. I kept thinking and thinking and boom! I thought of it! Miss, are you thinking what I'm thinking?"

Since Informative Language is the language of schooling, one would expect to notice what the researcher confirmed. This form of language was primarily observed in the classroom setting and not in the cafeteria, the hallways, or the playground. It appears that this form of language is developed by children as a tool for learning, but is elicited by teachers in the classroom setting and not necessarily by others in other situations.

It is the conclusion of the researcher that the children in the classrooms at the elementary school had language development in the full *range* of categories, Instrumental, Regulatory, Interactional, Personal, Imaginative, Heuristic, and Informative. They had the ability to express themselves in order to satisfy needs or desires; to control the behavior of others; to establish and define social relationships; to express individuality and personality; to create; to explore, investigate, to acquire knowledge and to understanding; and to communicate information. Although Standard English was not the general language of the area, the children possessed adequate language for effective communication.

Vocabulary development did not match the Standard English used and required in school. This was what the researcher has termed the *depth* of language development and usage. It was this deficiency in development that caused the children problems in expressing themselves well in school discussions and written assignments. According to Hart and Risley, this is the deficiency caused by living in poverty.[12] This is the deficiency that cannot be fully remediated by schools. This is the deficiency that contributes to these children being at risk for failure in school and for living in poverty as adults.

Schools are obligated to extend the opportunities for children to use language to learn. Pinnell and Matlin found that the key to positive change in language education was increasing the professional knowledge and practical skills of teachers.[13] Teachers must recognize that children are active learners, increasing their understanding through investigation and construction of meaning by using language. This process is assisted and affected by interaction with others. Learning must be built upon activities that allow investigation and collaboration.

Learning to accommodate the types of interactional structures with which students are familiar will enhance the language situations so students communicate comfortably. It is important to remember that children are being prepared to live in a multicultural world and they will have to function efficiently in a variety of situations. Therefore, as Pinnell states,

> Exploring the teacher's role involves developing sensitivity to the subtle communications through which the teacher shows the child what is valued in the learning situation. . . . They need opportunities to listen to themselves and to children talking and to look at the meanings and intentions behind the way they use language. . . . Helping children develop effective language use in school environments requires that we give at least as much attention to function as we do to the form and structure of language.[14]

"Children are naturally curious. When given an environment which allows for questions, exploration, and discovery, they interpret their experiences with what they know."[15] Once teachers have increased their sensitivity to the range of language functions used in their classrooms and in the school, several things happen. They have information on children to support instructional strategies to develop language, they can talk specifically about each child, and they can effectively plan instructional activities.

Notes

1. Rubin, D. (2000). *Teaching elementary language arts: A balanced approach* (6th Ed.). Boston, MA: Allyn & Bacon. p xxv.

2. National Center for Education Statistics (1999). *Urban schools: The challenge of location and poverty.* Washington, DC: U.S. Department of Education, Institute of Education Sciences.

3. The Annie E. Casey Foundation (2000). *Kids count census data analysis.* Baltimore, MD: Population Reference Bureau. Retrieved 3/8/04 from http://www.aecf.org/cgi-bin/aeccensus.cgi.

4. McKinney-Vento homeless education assistance act of 2001. House Rule 1. Public Law 107-110. Signed into law 1/08/2002, effective 7/01/2002.

5. Halliday, M.A.K. (1973). The functional basis of language. In Bernstein (Ed.), *Class, codes, and control, volume 2. Applied studies toward a sociology of language.* Boston, MA: Routledge & Kegan Paul, 343-366.

Halliday, M.A.K. (1975). *Learning how to mean: Explorations in the development of language.* London, England: Edward Arnold Ltd.

6. Pinnell, G.S. (1996). Ways to look at the functions of children's language. In Power & Hubbard (Eds.), *Language development, A reader for teachers.* Englewood Cliffs, NJ: Prentice-Hall, Inc., 146-154.

7. Pinnell, G.S. (2001). Language in primary classrooms. *Theory into practice,* 14(5). 318.

8. Pinnell 1996, 147

9. Ibid.

10. Ibid.

11. Ibid., 148.

12. Hart, B. & Risley T.R. (1995). *Meaningful differences in the everyday experiences of young American children.* Baltimore, MD: Paul H. Brookes Publishing Co.

13. Pinnell, G.S. & Matlin M.L. (Eds.) (1989). *Teachers and research, language learning in the classroom.* Newark, DE: International Reading Association.

14. Pinnell (2001). 326-327.

15. Smith-Burke, M.T. (1985). Reading and talking: Learning through interaction. In Jaggar & Smith-Burke (Eds.), *Observing the language learner.* Newark, DE: International Reading Association and Urbana, IL: National Council of Teachers of English, 199.

Chapter 8
Student/Teacher Interactions

Children who are not spoken to by live and responsive adults will not learn to speak properly. Children who are not answered will stop asking questions. They will become incurious. And children who are not told stories and who are not read to will have few reasons for wanting to learn to read.
Gail Haley[1]

When children are treated with respect, they conclude that they deserve respect and hence develop self-respect. When children are treated with acceptance, they develop self-acceptance; when they are cherished, they conclude that they deserve to be loved, and they develop self-esteem.
Stephanie Martson[2]

"Children grow into the intellectual life around them."[3] Vygotsky's theory is that the intellectual life is connected to and influenced by the social environment and interactions. Therefore, the intellectual is also relational and emotional. He believed this social nature of the intellect gives language a special and specific role to fulfill. By observing teachers, Johnston found that there were "subtle ways in which they built emotionally and relationally healthy learning communities. . . . Talk is the central tool of their trade. With it they mediate children's activity and experience, and help them make sense of learning, literacy, life, and themselves."[4]

The teacher must help children create meaning from what they say and do and help convey that meaning to others. The teacher "imputes intentions and offers possible worlds, positions, and identities."[5] Language carries information about the speaker, the listener and the relationship between them. Halliday has termed these the *ideational* and *interpersonal* dimensions of our speech.[6]

Language research has examined the explicitness of the language used by teachers.[7] There is information that students need that is best learned from their teacher. However, teachers must recognize the background children bring to any learning activity. They must not assume students know concepts not yet taught and discussed. Marie Clay found that the questions teachers ask indicate that the teacher often assumes that students have background knowledge they do not actually possess; and, therefore, the students cannot answer the questions.[8] Donaldson found that the more proficient a teacher is in a subject, the more chance there is that there will be a gap between the teacher and the learner.[9] This also means that the teaching may be more difficult. Although teachers must be direct and explicit in their instruction, they must take care that they do not ignore or dismiss input from students. They must also allow students to assume much of the responsibility for learning. Research found that the best and most effective teachers do not spend a lot of time telling. Instead, they have classrooms that allow and encourage student collaboration, exploration, brainstorming, and problem solving.[10]

Johnston contends that speech is action and that language "actually creates realities and invites identities."[11] Thus, when teachers complement students on their efforts, students begin to see themselves as capable and successful. Davies and Harre state that language establishes relationships.[12] The way teachers talk may either establish them as the *givers of information,* or as *partners and collaborators* with students in the learning process. The change is from the teacher being the "sage on the stage" to becoming the "guide on the side." This is a powerful shift in the teaching/learning relationship, empowering students to be responsible for their own learning.

Over one hundred hours of observation in the homeless shelter classroom were done. Teacher/student interactions were recorded and transcribed. These were analyzed using the categories described in *Choice Words, How Our Language Affects Children's Learning.*[13] Since the words teachers use with their students have an enormous impact on how students think about themselves as learners and how they work toward becoming independent, self-directed, purposeful, and successful in their learning, this analysis attempted to find and identify examples of teacher talk that accomplished these ends. "I focus on those things teachers say (and don't say) whose combined effect changes the literate lives of their students,"[14]

The six categories developed by Johnston for analysis of classroom interactions are: 1) Noticing and Naming, 2) Identity, 3) Agency and Becoming Strategic, 4) Flexibility and Transfer, 5) Knowing, and 6) Democratic Learning Community.[15]

Noticing and Naming

Noticing and Naming is a critical part of communication and is vitally necessary to being able to participate in particular activities. Teachers must help children notice important details and patterns so they can use this knowledge in appropriate ways for learning in different content areas. Harre and Gillet found that knowledge is gained by noticing things in context. Then, once one begins to notice these things, it is extremely difficult not to continue to do so.[16] As has been shown in previous chapters, the children in the shelter had acquired language and had a remarkable ability to use it. They could tell jokes, interact, gate keep, pretend, acquire and share knowledge. However, they were not always aware of the intricacies of language and its uses. It is the teachers' responsibility to help students notice language, its uses, and its effects on thinking. Examples of teacher talk that assist students in the process of noticing are:

Did you notice . . . ?
Look what you can do all by yourselves.
This is what I heard you doing during this activity/discussion.
Let's evaluate how it went. What went well? Where were the problems?
What kinds of questions did you have?
What are you seeing?
What patterns do you see?
What did you expect? What is unexpected?

These types of teacher questions and comments help students learn the significant features of the world, themselves, and others. It will then impact how they interact with each other and their world. Therefore, such teacher talk is necessary in a productive teaching/learning environment. However, in the hours of taped interactions in the classroom with the most disadvantaged students, little such talk was evident. One example in the *Noticing and Naming* category occurred during a mathematics lesson on multiplication.

Teacher: But you also should write the answer to your math problem. O.K. Here you're putting only one check. Why are you doing that? How many checks should you have?
Student: Four.
Teacher: And how many boxes?
Student: Five.
Teacher: O.K. 4 X 5 is what?
Student: 20.
Teacher: 20. So we need how many checks?
Student: 4 in one box and 4 in the other box, plus the boxes of three.
Teacher: No. You're just going to do four checks in the first five boxes because four times five is twenty. Do you see what I mean?
Teacher: We came up with the correct answer over there. This should be the number of checks and this is the number of boxes that the checks would go in.
Student: O.K.
Teacher: Say, Jesse. Do you understand? Four checks times five is twenty. So put four checks in each box. No, not scribble lines like that-checks, O.K. Now do four. You don't have to make them big, you can make them little like that. There you go. There you are. That's better. And then you go back and write your answers here.

This interaction was a brief step toward helping students answer the questions, "What are you noticing? Are you seeing any patterns?" It helped students focus on the things they observed and created to begin to see how these patterns made sense in the larger framework of their knowledge. This interaction, however, would have been much more powerful if the teacher had explicitly pointed out or questioned children directly about the patterns they created and if she had caused the children to notice these patterns more overtly. The patterns being created by making checks in the boxes should have led students to a better understanding of how multiplication problems operate and how they can be solved. Although implied in the teacher's questions, these patterns were not pointed out or directly identified. Such explicitness would have facilitated having all students notice and name them and then put the concepts to use in further problem solving.

Identity

Identity is the second category of interaction that Johnston uses for analysis. He said,

> Building an identity means coming to see in ourselves the characteristics of particular categories (and roles) of people and developing a sense of what it feels like to be that sort of person and belonging in certain social spaces. . . . Teachers' comments can offer them, and nudge them toward, productive identities.[17]

Examples of these types of comments are:

> What a great (title of profession) you are.
> I'm proud of you and you should be of yourself.
> How or what are you doing as a (title of profession)?
> What have you learned as a (title of profession)?

To answer these questions, the student must think of him/herself in the stated role. This requires understanding what that role is and how such a professional would act or react. When students become more aware of possibilities for themselves, it can effect their participation in learning activities. As Johnston said, "Learning science, writing, mathematics, and so forth in this manner breaks the division between school and 'the real world,' a division that limits the power of children's learning." [18]

Unfortunately, in the over 100 hours of taped interactions in the classroom with homeless children, this type of conversation was never recorded. There was a great deal of telling students how to behave, but not how to identify with a greater goal for learning. The following exchanges happened during a science lesson.

Teacher: Well, what else can we do (that animals can't)?

Boy: Read, write, and learn. Animals can't read or write or learn. But they can breathe, they can see, they can hear. But they can't learn.

Teacher: Let's see. For one thing we are capable of a wider range of movement than most animals. The human hand, in particular, can do anything from grasping a hammer to playing the piano. Another reason we are special is our brain. It is so highly evolved that we have been able to think about other things besides the need to survive on a day-to-day basis. We have developed.

Lori: Miss, my sister is over there and she's suppose to be over here.

Teacher: I know she is, but I'm not gonna take time aside from the lecture, OK, to get her. So I want you to listen OK, Lori. I need you to listen please, OK. We have developed a culture that includes language.

This discussion was the perfect opportunity for the teacher to help students begin to think of themselves as scientists and get them more involved and active in the learning process. However, she let that opportunity pass to focus on her "lecture." She was so intent on covering what she had planned, that she did not even acknowledge the excellent contribution made to the discussion by the boy. His comments were directly related to the teacher's point regarding the differences between the human brain and that of animals, but she did not recognize it at all. Her only deviation from her purpose was the exchange with Lori regarding Lori's little sister who was not engaged in the discussion at all. It should be noted that the little sister was a kindergartner and this discussion was beyond her comprehension and, therefore, she had chosen to go to another part of the room and play. She was not being disruptive or a distraction to anyone except Lori until the teacher brought it to everyone's attention with her comments. Like many others in the hours of observation, this was a wonderful opportunity which was missed; and, therefore, the neediest children got the least productive learning situation.

Agency and Becoming Strategic

Agency and Becoming Strategic is Johnston's third category for analysis of student/teacher interactions. Agency is the understanding that the environment responds to personal actions.[19] Researchers have found this to be a basic desire of people.[20] Skinner, Zimmer-Gembeck and Connell[21] even found that people who do not see any relationship between their actions and what happens, develop depression and helplessness. Johnston said, "If nothing else, children should leave school with a sense that if they act, and act strategically, they can accomplish their goals. . . . Some teachers are very good at building a sense of agency in children."[22] Dyson said, "A child must have some version of, 'Yes, I imagine

I can do this.' And a teacher must also view the present child as competent and on that basis imagine new possibilities."[23]

The following are examples of the kind of language teachers use to help students develop their sense of agency.

"How did you figure that out?"[24]
What questions are still not answered?
How do you think you can get this done? What steps will you take?
What is your intent or audience for this piece of writing?
What things are you sure of and what do you still question?

In any learning activity, students must do a certain amount of *self-talk*. If the task is difficult or frustrating for them, their self-talk may be negative and may cause them to give up in frustration. If they try their hardest and cannot do it, the only thought may be, "I'm a failure." However, if they do not try their hardest and fail, they then have the psychological way out of saying, "If I had tried harder, I could have done it." Therefore, when children see themselves as failures at a task, they try less hard when approaching that task. Teachers must work at overcoming this negative self-talk by the encouragement and positive feedback they give students. They must notice their efforts, their successes (even if only partial ones) and help students begin to view themselves as capable. Teachers must help children to tell themselves they are actively engaged in successful learning experiences. This will influence their academic achievement.[25]

In the following exchange between Jesse and the teacher, there are glimpses of this type of teacher talk in which she tries to get Jesse to see himself as having background knowledge to bring to the discussion and as having the ability to make choices about how the activity is completed.

Teacher: Jesse, if you lived in Texas how would you get to Georgia? What states are those?
Jesse: This one's Mississippi and Alabama.
Teacher: Alabama. Well, let's try to pronounce this one right here, O.K. Let's see.
Jesse: Loui . . .
Teacher: .siana
Jesse: Louisiana
Teacher: Louisiana. Have you ever lived anywhere besides Texas?
Jesse: I lived in Ohio.
Teacher: You lived in Ohio. Well, that's a different state. Did you know that? Let's see. Can we find Ohio? That's pretty far from Texas.
Teacher: Well, let's see. So our shortest route do you think would be to go straight across this way.
Jesse: Yes.
Teacher: So if we lived in Texas and we're trying to get to Georgia, we

go this way?
Jesse: No, no. Go like this. Swim through here and then go right here.
Teacher: You're going to swim?
Teacher: Do you think you might get tired if you decided to swim from
Texas to Georgia?
Jesse: No, 'cause I'm strong!

Teacher: Let's see, Jesse, did you decide how you were going to get to
Georgia from Texas? Well, you can write #1 and then put the
states you'd have to go through, O.K. You'd write them in a
line. And then you'd be done answering that. So go ahead and
do that.

So much more could have been said during the interaction to empower
Jesse to acknowledge his background and help him see himself as a capable
learner of geography. Just some more overt recognition of his input would have
strengthened these ideas and concepts considerably. However, the teacher may
not have recognized these possibilities herself and so was unable to convey this
to Jesse. Again, so many opportunities were missed because of lack of training,
skill, experience, and insight on the part of the teacher.

Flexibility and Transfer or Generalizing

Flexibility and Transfer or Generalizing is understanding that what is learned in
one area of life or part of school is used in other areas and that there are strong
connections between what is learned in school and the "real" world. This is
vitally important to making the most of what is learned and for being the most
effective in learning new skills. The following are examples of teacher talk to
encourage flexibility and transfer:

How would you do this as a (title of profession)?
How else might this be done?
Is this like anything else you have ever seen or done?
Ask yourself, "What if . . .?"

Flexible thinking involves expanding students' imagination with what-if
questions. Teachers must help children try out their learning and strategies and
help them make adaptations and adjustments where needed. This promotes abstract thinking, problem solving, and exploration of differences. "These abilities
are fundamental to both productive individual choice and to negotiating collaboratively productive meanings and solutions as required for democratic living."[26]
The learning environment must be one where it is safe to try things out, to explore, and to seek different solutions.
In the following example from the shelter classroom, a student really has a
breakthrough in understanding the concept of multiplication. Her excitement

about this is evident in the transcript.

> Teacher: O.K. What's 7 X 1?
> Student: 7.
> Teacher: O.K.
> Student: Hey! There's a mistake in here, Teacher.
> Teacher: There is?
> Student: Yes. This one.
> Teacher: 3 X 7 is what?
> Student: 3 X 7 is different because we ain't doing the three.
> Teacher: I know but you're doing sevens.
> Student: But seven first!
> Teacher: No, it can be in any order. See on number 2 how it's 6 X 7?
>   O.K. What's 6 X 7?
> Student: Okay, then it can go in any order when you're doing multi-
>   plying? Wow, cool!

This small window of insight is a great example of Flexibility and Transfer. A student began to understand how things operated and could then apply that to additional learning activities. This student went on to do the rest of the page of multiplication problems with no trouble at all. She had learned the multiplication tables through 4 and so as she came to each example of multiplying 7, she found the smaller of the two numbers and put it first in the equation. Often the example then became one of the combinations she had already memorized. She was so proud of herself and really began to see herself as capable of doing mathematics.

Knowing

Knowing involves using language that helps students take a more active role in their own learning. Rogoff and Toma state:

> Learning to act as a recipient of information and to display receipt of the infor-
> mation . . . [is not the same as] building on ideas in a shared endeavor [in
> which] participants' roles can vary widely, such as leading a shared inquiry,
> playing around with an idea together, or closely following other people's lines
> of thought.[27]

Higgins, Stegall and Crist say teachers "need to encourage student question-ing because such an act is natural in every setting outside of the school setting, and should thus be so in the school setting if lifelong learning is a true goal."[28]

These are examples of teacher talk which produces knowing:

Let me see if I can summarize what you have said or written.
What questions could we start with so we can seek the answers?

I like the way you clarified that.

"That's a very interesting way of looking at it. I hadn't thought about it that way. I'll have to think about it some more."[29]

How did you know that and how can we check it out?

Is that a fact or an opinion?

"Is that an observation or conjecture?"[30]

The following exchange between Lorraine and the teacher happened when they were discussing how to solve some multiplication problems by drawing pictures as illustrations for the operation. The students were to put checks representing one digit of the equation into boxes representing the other digit of the equation. Then they would be able to count the number of check marks to determine the answer to the multiplication problem. After several examples had been done, Lorraine encountered a problem with zero as one of the digits.

Lorraine: These check marks they can go . . . I get mixed up. I'm gonna just put..

Teacher: Do you understand them, Lorraine?

Lorraine: Oh! We don't put none in here.

Teacher: Well, how many checks does that tell you?

Lorraine: Zero. And none in five boxes.

Teacher: Right. So do you put any checks?

Lorraine: No.

Teacher: O.K. So you see how you can think through the problem to figure out how to work it. What if the zero was in the place of the second number?

Lorraine: You would just do it the same way with checks in zero boxes. I get it – ha, ha!!

Teacher: Let's see if you can help the others then because you understand it so well.

Lorraine then went around helping other students with the problems which she had "mastered." This exchange is an excellent example which shows the power of helping students brainstorm and figure out what they already know in order to learn new information, strategies, or operations. It is a powerful teaching tool that, sadly, was used much too seldom with the children at the homeless shelter classroom.

A Democratic Learning Community

An Evolutionary, Democratic Learning Community involves the social relationships within the classroom that are a large part of students' learning. Children learn better in a supportive environment in which they can risk trying out new strategies and concepts and stretching themselves intellectually. These learning environments require structure to "help each other and check each other's tendencies to purely idiosyncratic or self-interested thinking."[31] Some teachers are very gifted in building learning communities in which individuals feel valued and supported, and that maintain productive learning. Children must have these experiences if they are to know how to construct their own learning environments. Tsuchida and Lewis found that even when students worked in groups, they rarely worked *as* a group or shared ideas to work toward a common goal.[32] Examples of teacher comments that can create a caring and respectful learning environment community are:

> We work together here and help each other.
> How would you feel if you were in his/her place?
> Who can share a compliment for a classmate?
> Does anyone have another way of thinking about that or have any other opinions about this subject?
> "What are you thinking? Stop and talk to your neighbor about it."[33]
> "You managed to figure that out with each other's help."[34]

> Teachers need to provide choice and develop authentic tasks. . . . Providing choice promotes active learning and shifts the locus of control to the learner while authentic tasks . . . are logical outgrowths of the natural learning systems.[35]

In the classroom with the homeless children, creation of a democratic learning environment was not often done. However, a few examples were found in the taped observations. The following examples fit the category of teacher talk that builds a democratic learning environment:

> Teacher: They're doing good. They're almost done, except for Laura because she didn't want to listen when I was giving the explanation so she is not being able to do the worksheet.
> Teacher: Class, what are you doing? Stop and talk to your partner about it. Someone tell Laura how you did it.
> Teacher: Thank you for your hard work.

This exchange helped Laura get back on task and helped the other students recognize their concept development. It made everyone feel proud of their "hard work" because the teacher had acknowledged it. Students are more inclined to repeat behaviors that get positive reinforcement from the teacher. This interchange also helped students see that sharing and discussing processes and concepts with each other was beneficial to all learning.

Another example occurred when students were supposed to be working independently in learning centers:

> Student: Oh! I don't know my centers. Miss, how do you do this?

Teacher: O.K. Let's read the directions together. Who wants to read
the directions?

Student: Me.

Teacher: O.K. Go ahead Lorraine.

Lorraine: Circle every seventh number and use the circled numbers to
solve each multiplication problem.

Teacher: O.K. So we're going to do multiples of seven, right? Because
that would be every seventh number. So if we count
seven—Count—one, two, three, four, five, six, seven. Now
let's count seven more. After seven, count what it would it
be. Let's all count together.

Student: It would be 14. And the next one would be 21. Miss, I got the
hang of this. Ohhh!

The teacher's support for reading the directions together and having students help each other empowered the student to "get it." That excitement of ac-
complishment was then shared with the rest of the class and all felt a sense of
pride.

In creating a democratic learning community, it is important for the teacher
to share responsibilities with the students and make the students believe they
make valuable contributions to the learning activities. In the following interchange, the teacher really does the opposite of this when talking to the students
about their coming trip to Sea World. It is really a harangue regarding all the
work she has to do to get the trip organized. It probably should not have been
shared with the students at all. However, here it is:

Teacher: And the ones that behave do know that you don't have to listen to me. Jesse, sit. I just took 50 minutes which is most of
an hour trying to get a fieldtrip approved for the end of the
year. That takes a lot of time, it takes money, it takes food, it
takes transportation. A note has to be sent home to parents
for permission. We just can't say, "Oh, well! Tomorrow
when you come in we're all gonna load the van and go to
Sea World." It would be nice.

Student: Yeah, it would.

Teacher: But, we can't do that. It takes planning and I am not going to
take my time—that was my 45 minutes out of class, that
was my free time, that was my conference time to talk to
parents or what have you. I could have just gone over to the
coffee machine, made some coffee for later on. I have
plenty of work to do. But I didn't. I spent it on the phone—
on hold—talking to people at Sea World. Talking to Bill
(the Director of the shelter) seeing if we can come up with
the money to take all of you. It costs a lot of money to go to
a nice place like that, but it's worth it. It's worth it for me to

be able to have you all go to Sea World to see Shamu and
the shows and stuff.

Student: How much, Miss, does it cost?

Teacher: Almost two-hundred dollars. Twelve dollars a person. O.K.
So let's see this. Fifteen times twelve. We have how many
heads in here?

Student: Fifteen.

Teacher: You sure?

Student: Yes.

Teacher: Twelve dollars each—plus we're gonna take the chaperones.
So say me and Ms. Gonzales and two other people. So that
would be fifteen students, plus me, Ms.Gonzales. O.K. we'll
pay our own way. But I know that we're gonna have one
additional parent that we're gonna have to pay for. So we're
gonna have fifteen, say sixteen, times twelve. So 6 X 2?

Student: It's twelve.

Teacher: And 6 X 1?

Students: Six.

Teacher: Times 2?

Student: 2.

Teacher: And 1 X 1?

Student: 1.

Teacher: $192.00 dollars.

Student: Whoa!!!!!

Teacher: That's just to get us in the door. That's not no food, the gaso-
line for the van, no spending money for souvenirs, that's
just the trip to get in the door, to go to the shows, and I'm
not gonna, even gonna, let you go into the waterpark because it's only open 'til six and we're only gonna have like,
what, three hours after the Shamu show and I want you to
go to some of the other shows and, you know, you don't
have to go into that arcade part either. That just drives me
nuts—to take my kids to Sea World so they can play pinball
machines. That's not why we go to Sea World. And my kids
are 13 and 17 and I don't let them go into the arcades at Sea
World or Fiesta Texas. That's not why we're there. If we
want to play pinball machines, we can go to a grocery store.

Student: Or River Center.

Teacher: O.K. Or River Center. I mean there's quarter pinball, you
know, that's not why we're there. O.K. We're there to go on
the rides, we're there to go on the shows, we're there to go,
you know. I realize that the water park is fun and everything, but we're not gonna go into the water because there's
not enough adults and something could happen, and, you
know, I'm just not gonna let you do that. But that involves

renting lockers, taking towels, and change of clothes, and we're just not gonna do that. O.K. But nobody can go if they don't behave. I'm not taking anybody anywhere and spending all that money if you don't know how to behave.

Student: Miss, we know how to behave.

Teacher: Well, we'll see. I'm not so sure! I know for probably sure that some of you won't get to go because you don't behave.

At this point, the conversation began to move in a different direction and other subjects were addressed. However, in watching the students at that moment, it was clear to this observer that they were much less excited about the possibility of going to Sea World. In fact, several of the students later expressed concern that they might not be allowed to go. No time was ever spent learning about the animals they would see when they went on the field trip. There was never any brainstorming regarding the concepts they would be exposed to or the learning that would take place while on the trip. This was an excellent opportunity for the students at all levels to learn more about ocean life, their environment, and even social aspects of going out to such a public place. However, the opportunity was missed and the children did not gain all they could have from the trip even though they had a wonderful time and thoroughly enjoyed the day. These children, who have so little opportunity to experience such activities, should be afforded the richest experiences possible. However, if teachers are not aware, prepared, and skilled, these opportunities will be missed and the children will be cheated out of enhanced learning experiences.

> One of the greatest gifts you can share with your students is to help them understand the democratic process by creating a civic culture in your classroom. A civic culture is a public space where ideas are shared, differences of opinion are honored and where all citizens are committed to creating a consensus. Classroom democracy is built on the concept of inclusion and giving voice to each and every student.[36]

This may be even more important for students who are disadvantaged because of their living conditions, their lack of security in their home or family situation, and/or their constant mobility and having to adjust to new and different placements in schools. Having their voices heard and valued can be an important aspect of helping them see possibilities beyond their current situation and helping them look toward a future where they can be successful and achieve a better life for themselves.

There is a heavy responsibility on each teacher to provide students with a place to be heard and valued. "Teachers are the weavers of the social fabric. . . . Take each student as a thread to be woven into the social fabric and treasure him or her delicately as you weave your small corner of the social tapestry which is democracy."[37]

Notes

1. Haley, G. (1985). In Andrews, Biggs, & Seidel (Eds.). *The Columbia world of quotations.* New York, NY: Columbia University Press. Retrieved 12/13/2006 from http://history.enotes.com/famous-quotes/children-who-are-not-spoken-to-by-live-and>.

2. Martson, S. (2005) *The balancing act.* Issue 7, July 2005. Retrieved 1/30/2007 from http://www.stephaniemarston.com/newsletters/july05.html.

3. Vygotsky, L.S. (1978). *Mind in society: The development of higher psychological processes.* Cambridge, MA: Harvard University Press. 88.

4. Johnston, P.H. (2004). *Choice words, how our language affects children's learning.* Portland, ME: Stenhouse Publishers. 4.

5. Ibid., 5.

6. Halliday, M.A.K. (1994). *An introduction to functional grammar.* 2nd Ed. London, England: Edward Arnold.

7. Delpit, L. (1988). The silenced dialogue: power and pedagogy in educating other people's children. *Harvard educational review*, 58(3), 280-298.

   Pressley, M.; Allington, R.L.; Wharton-MacDonald, R.; Collins-Black, C.; & Morrow, L. (2001). *Learning to read: Lessons for exemplary first-grade classrooms.* New York, NY: Guilford.

   Pressley, M. & Woloshyn, V. (1995). *Cognitive strategy instruction that really improves children's academic performance*, 2nd Ed. Cambridge, MA: Brookline Books.

8. Clay, M.M. (1991). *Becoming literate: The construction of inner control.* Portsmouth, NH: Heinemann.

9. Donaldson, M. (1978). *Children's minds.* New York, NY: W. W. Norton.

10. Taylor, B.M.; Peterson, D.S.; Pearson, P.D.; & Rodriguez, M. (2002). Looking inside classrooms: Reflecting on the 'how' as well as the 'what' in effective reading instruction. *The reading teacher*, 56, 70-79.

11. Johnston, 9.

12. Davies, B. & Harre, R. (1999). Positioning and personhood. In Harre and Langenhove (Eds.), *Positioning theory: Moral contexts of intentional action.* Oxford, England: Blackwell, 32-52.

13. Johnston

14. Ibid., 2.

15. Ibid.

16. Harre, R. & Gillet, G. (1994). *The discursive mind.* Thousand Oaks, CA: Sage.

17. Johnston, 23.

18. Ibid., 24.

19. Ibid.

20. Bandura, A. (1996). *Self-Efficacy: The exercise of control.* New York, NY: Freeman.

    Bruner, J. (1994). The 'remembered' self. In Neisser & Fivush, (Eds.), *The remembering self: Construction and accuracy in the self-narrative.* Cambridge, MA: Cambridge University Press, 41-54.

    Harre & Gillet

    Skinner, E.A.; Zimmer-Gembeck, M.J.; & Connell, J.P. (1998). Individual differences and the development of perceived control (254). *Monographs of the society for research in child development*, 63, 2-3.

21. Skinner, Zimmer-Gembeck & Connell

22. Johnston, 29.

23. Dyson, A.H. (1999). Coach Bombay's kids learn to write: Children's appro-

priation of media material for school literacy. *Research in the teaching of English*, 33(4), 396-397.

24. Johnson, 31.

25. Johnston, P.H. & Winograd, P.N. (1985). Passive failure in reading. *Journal of reading behavior* 17(4), 279-301.

Nicholls, J.G. (1989). *The competitive ethos and democratic education*. Cambridge, MA: Harvard University Press.

Nolen-Hoeksema, S.; Girus, J.S.; & Seligman, M.E.P. (1986). Learned helplessness in children: A longitudinal study of depression, achievement, and explanatory style. *Journal of personality and social psychology*, 51, 435-442.

26. Johnston, 47-48.

27. Rogoff, B. & Toma, C. (1997). Shared thinking: Community and institutional variations. *Discourse processes*, 475.

28. Higgins, Stegall & Crist (2004). The neglected half of teaching. In Flores, Hufford & Starlin (Eds). *Educating for peace: Cherishing diversity. Journal of interdisciplinaryeducation* 6(1). San Antonio, TX: North America Chapter of the World Council for Curriculum and Instruction.76.

29. Johnston, P.H. & Backer. J. (2002). Inquiry and a good conversation: 'I learn a lot from them'. In Allington & Johnston (Eds.), R*eading to learn: Lessons from exemplary fourth-grade classrooms*. New York, NY: Guilford, 42.

30. Ibid., 47.

31. Young, R. (1992). *Critical theory and classroom talk*. Philadelphia, PA: Multilingual Matters. 8.

32. Tsuchida, I. & Lewis, C. (1996). Responsibility and learning: Some preliminary hypotheses about Japanese elementary classrooms. In Rohlen & LeTender (Eds.), *Teaching and learning in Japan*. New York, NY: Cambridge University Press, 190-212.

33. Johnson, 71.

34. Ibid., 71.

35. Higgins, Stegall & Crist, 76.

36. Cookson, P.W. (2005). Creating a civic culture. *Teaching K-8*. February 2005 (10). Norwalk, CT: Early Years, Inc. ,19.

37. Ibid., 19.

Chapter 9
Dreams and Reality

Children cannot eat rhetoric and they cannot be sheltered by com-
missions. I don't want to see another commission that studies the
needs of kids. We need to help them.
Marian Wright Edelman[1]

Dreams

One day while walking through the hallway of the elementary school in the housing project, I found two large posters on the wall near the library. One of these posters had been written on by parents and the other by the children in the school. The poster written and illustrated by the parents was entitled, "My Dream to my Kids." The following were the things on that poster which have been grouped by the topic they addressed.

- Pictures of dream houses, yard, swings, clothesline, individual bed-rooms
- My Dream—they go to colleges—My Dream.
- For all my kids to have a college education.
- My dream is to see my daughters finish high school, graduate, and proceed to college.
- My dreams is for my children to go to colleges.
- To be able to see our kids graduate!
- Keep kids in school and off the streets.
- My dreams are for my children to finish high school and go to college and get good jobs and to live happy lifes. My dream for me is to grow old with my husband.
- I want a better life for my kids and all other kids in the world!
- Never run out of money.
- Get a job and get off welfare. Learn to support my own family.
- Better living for my family.
- Give unconditional love to our children when they give us bad re-

port—To teachers that don't understand our children—To Parents
that works 8 hours—To parents that don't have no interest to their
own children's education—To teenager that are out in streets

- No trushing down town. (trashing)
- Make peace—no more hate.
- For ever one to believe in God! It would be a better world.
- Good hospitals

These seem to be *universal* dreams that parents everywhere share for their
children, wanting them to have a better future and a better world to live in. Parents'
desire for their children to have a better life is often centered around the idea of
getting a good education. Even though most of these parents had not gone to
college and many had not even completed high school, they believed that a good
education was the path for their children out of the projects, poverty and away from
crime.

Gary Blair, "The GoalsGuy," has suggested goals for the development of
children's lives.[2] These are the ten things parents should work on to build into the
life of their children.

Goal 1: Positive Self-Image. Parents and teachers must tell children that they
have worth. Children must be encouraged at every opportunity if they are to
develop a positive self-image.

Goal 2: Sense of Independence. Parents and teachers should help children
know that they can come to them for guidance, love and advice, but that they must
develop into their own person.

Goal 3: Sense of Dependence on God. The best way to help children learn this
is to see it modeled in the lives of the adults around them.

Goal 4: Responsibility for Actions and Consequences. Adults must model
responsible behavior with no excuses ever. Then children will know how to
develop this characteristic in their own lives.

Goal 5: Recognize and Embrace Their Potential. Helping children know what
they are capable of is vital to their fulfilling their potential. The adults in the child's
life must help them explore the possibilities.

Goal 6: Use Their Ability. Helping children explore options and try things out
in a safe environment is necessary for the development of their abilities.

Goal 7: Hope. Blair says, "The best chance for a productive and prosperous
future is to give your children an understanding of hope. Goal-oriented people are
those who learn to live in hope because they are always moving toward an
objective."[3]

Goal 8: Happiness. Parents and teachers should teach children that problems
can be turned into opportunities for learning. Learning and growing then lead to
happiness with problems solved and new insights gained.

Goal 9: Good Character. Blair says, "This quality is essential to achieving
personal success and fulfillment in life."[4]

Goal 10: Sense of Fun. According to Blair, "Fun is the fabric of happy memories, the icing on the cake of life. . . . Let your child see you laughing and enjoying life. This will, in affect, tickle the toes of their soul as well."[5]

These dreams and goals are shared by parents at all socio-economic levels and in all areas of our country. The real difference lies in the parents' ability to provide for or facilitate the development of that better future and better world for their children. In her book, *A Framework for Understanding Poverty*, Ruby Payne demonstrates how people at various socio-economic levels develop very different skills for their environment in order to successfully operate and survive.[6] Knowing how to help your child get into college and how to choose the appropriate college for their interests is easily developed at the higher socio-economic levels. Parents at the lowest levels are simply trying to provide on a day-to-day basis for the basic needs of their children. However, it is obvious that the hearts' desire of parents at *all* levels is to see their children succeed in whatever way success is measured in their culture and socio-economic level. Parents want the future for their children to be better than the life the parent has had.

The dreams of the parents at the elementary school in the project and the goals given by Blair are wonderful and important. However, in his Hierarchy of Needs, Maslow classified the Physiological, Safety, Belonging and Love, and Esteem Needs as *Deficit Needs* which must be met before the *Being Need* for Self-Actualization can even be contemplated.[7]

Figure 9.1[8]

Maslow's Hierarchy of Needs

When the parents' dreams and Blair's goals are viewed in light of Maslow's Hierarchy of Needs, it is clear that they lie in the realm of the *Being Need*, Self-Actualization. Unless the more basic *Deficit Needs* of the parents and children living in extreme poverty are met, these dreams and goals will remain out of reeach and unfulfilled.

The poster on the opposite wall of the elementary school had been made by the children in the school and was entitled "Dreams for our World." The following were the things on that poster which have been grouped by the topics they addressed.

Safety

- No more bad things.
- I have a dream that there are no more drive bys, or shooting. I want people to love each other. We should fight with words instead of guns.
- No more fighting.
- No fighting in daycare.
- Please stop killing children in school.
- I have a dream that there are no more guns or violence in our schools.
- Children will be safe evrywhere.
- No more violence. (written 2 times this way)
- No more violence—peace.
- Stop violence.
- Say no to violence.
- No more gangs, fighting, or violence.
- I have a dream that there are no more bullets and no more guns.
- No more drive by shooting.
- No more drive-by.
- No drive by's.
- Stop the gangs. (written 2 times this way)
- No gangs.
- No more dropping out of school. And no more selling guns in stores.
- Drug free people.
- Say no to drugs.
- No more drugs in the world.
- Do not steal in the store.
- You can leave the keys in the car.
- No more robing. (robbing)
- People will be honest.
- People will be honest and leave car alone.
- People can leave their keys in the door.
- People can sleep outside.

Eliminating Poverty

- No more poor people.
- Homes for homeless people.
- Homes for homeless people, friendly walking.
- Houses for everyone.

- Food, clothing, shelter, ed.
- Enough food for everyone.
- Help people on streets.
- Our world needs more camps to keep people off the streets.

Improving the Neighborhood

- Neighbors who help each other.
- The neighbors will talk to each other.
- Good schools—graduating and getting jobs.
- Clean neighborhood and streets.
- Help others.
- Families that are happy and care about each other.
- Our world needs more churches.
- Clean streets and clean schools and friendly people.
- We all love each other.
- Friendship.
- Respect.
- Freedom.
- Love.

Making the World Better

- Let's help save the world.
- Clean world.
- No more trash.
- Clean houses.
- Cars that don't pollute.
- The world will be beautiful tomorrow.
- Gardens.
- Beautiful gardens.
- Lots of trees.
- Bas cit ball cort. (basketball court)
- Parks where we can play.
- Pretty houses without writing. Clean houses with no graffiti.
- No grafatti. (graffiti)
- Clean air and water.
- Recycling.
- No more pollution.
- Clean oceans for whales.
- Good water.
- Lots of animals.
- Peace.
- Stop the wars.

These dreams very closely align with Maslow's Hierarchy of Needs[9]. These children lived with great need for food, shelter and safety, the lowest and most necessary level of Maslow's Hierarchy. Therefore, the dreams they voiced over 53% of the time were for these needs to be met. They could not dream of higher goals and objectives because these basic necessities were not being met. In the listing of dreams for their world, the children overwhelmingly expressed the desire for meeting the basic needs.

Maslow believed that violence and other evils occur when basic human needs are unmet.[10] People who are deprived of lower needs such as safety may defend themselves by violent means because of necessity, not because they enjoy violence. Meeting safety needs establishes stability and consistency in a chaotic world and provides the security of a home and family. People generally want law and order so they can feel safe enough to go for a walk in their neighborhood. Safety needs often motivate people to be religious because religions comfort us with the promise of a safe secure place after we die and leave the insecurity of this world.[11] Belonging and love is the third tier in the hierarchy. People have a desire to belong to groups, whether it be clubs, churches, families, or even gangs. In fact, children often turn to gangs for that feeling of belonging when this need is not met by their family, either intimate or extended. Even when the negative factors of gangs are considered, the need to belong and be loved and cared for will outweigh all the risks and cause children and youths to endure the initiation and face the dangers of membership to fulfill that need. Even though many children wrote that gangs should be eliminated and they did not want anything to do with gangs, a great many will succumb to the attraction of gang membership before they reach adulthood.

The *Deficit Needs* that Maslow identified are seen in the writings of the children in the elementary school in the housing project. Clearly, they express the fact that their very basic needs are not being met.

Reality

These are the dreams of the parents and children living in poverty. What is the reality of their future? Can their basic needs be met so they can strive toward satisfying their higher need for self-actualization? How can this be assured for the children living in poverty? The reality for them is that their basic needs may not be met; that they may continue to be hungry, frightened, homeless, unsafe and unloved. The data indicate that their future is less than the best and brightest.

A report from the Children's Defense Fund, *Children in Texas*, says that a child is born into poverty every 7 minutes, one is abused or neglected every 11 minutes, one dies before his first birthday every 4 hours, and a child or teen is killed by gunfire every day.[12] With first place representing the best state for children, Texas ranks 43rd among states in the percent of children who are poor. This is 1,309,919 children or 21.8 percent. These numbers from 2006 show an increase in the number living in poverty over 1999, when Texas reported 1,189,935 or 20.5 percent. Living in poverty does not allow one to fulfill those basic needs for food, shelter and safety that are vital to development of self-esteem and self-actualization.

When examining the dreams the parents have for their children, they repeatedly named finishing high school and going to college. However, the

Children's Defense Fund report indicates that 73 percent of fourth graders were reading below grade level and 67 percent of them were below grade level in math. This does not bode well for the prospects of finishing high school. In fact, the report shows that only 79.4 percent of students complete high school.[13] Children in the poorest families are 6 times as likely as children in more affluent families to drop out of high school. The Children's Defense Fund found that persistence and success in school are also impacted by absences. These absences are caused by many factors, but having unmet basic needs is one of the main causes.[14]

There are disparities in educational resources for minority and low-income children.[15] Research has shown that the resources that most effectively promote student achievement are quality teachers, smaller class sizes and access to high quality after-school programs, advanced curricula, and modern learning facilities. However, "significant disparities exist between wealthy, predominantly White communities, and those populated by poor and minority families, putting poor and minority children at significant academic disadvantage."[16] Having highly qualified teachers is one of the most significant factors in improving student achievement.[17] But, poor children have significantly less opportunity to have quality teachers and teaching.[18] This is because schools with the highest percentages of minority and low-income students are more likely to have beginning teachers and teachers who are teaching out of their field of expertise or certification.[19] In fact, the data in this report show that classes in high-poverty schools are 77 percent more likely to be assigned to an out-of-field teacher than are classes in more affluent schools. Teachers with master's degrees are less likely to teach in high poverty schools and the turnover rate is almost one third higher than the rate for all teachers in all schools.[20] The Commission found that this high turnover is caused by poor working conditions, including inadequate facilities, less availability of textbooks and supplies, fewer administrative supports, and larger class sizes. High turnover is a financial burden to school districts because it represents a loss of resources to the system. A Texas study estimated the cost of teacher turnover to be between $216 and $329 million each year.[21]

Having safe, smaller classes which are taught by highly qualified teachers is another factor leading to academic success for students. However, in high poverty schools, small class sizes are not equally available. The Children's Defense Fund found that 31 percent of high poverty classes had 25 or more students, while less than 22 percent of low poverty classes had 25 or more.[22]

The third factor in academic success is access to advanced curricula. According to a study by the National Center for Education Statistics, the rigor of coursework reflects the quality of education schools deliver.[23] However, they found that advanced curricula and high quality college preparation are not available to all on equal levels. The National Research Council analyzed data and found that minority students are only half as likely as Whites to be placed in classes for the gifted and talented. There are also much lower numbers of minority students in advanced math and science classes and fewer of these students take Advanced Placement examinations.[24]

The fourth factor contributing to academic success is quality school facilities. The National Center for Education Statistics found that schools with 50 percent or more minorities or 70 percent or more low-income are twice as likely to be overcrowded as schools whose students are less than 20 percent minorities. [25]

The Children's Defense Fund report also says that 12.6 percent of 16 to 19 year-olds are not enrolled in school and are not high school graduates and 19.1 percent are unemployed.[26] Not doing well in school and not finishing are highly correlated with juvenile crime. In 2003, Texas had 180,017 juveniles arrested and 11,231 children and teens in juvenile or adult correctional facilities. The total number of children and teens killed by firearms was 241. One hundred forty of these deaths were homicides, 84 were suicides, 15 were accidents, and 2 were unclassified. If children are to reach the goals their parents have dreamed for them, they must be lifted out of poverty.

The United States reduced its child poverty rate by 50 percent in the 1960s. However, since then, child poverty has increased because the national effort has been to try to improve economic security for the elderly rather than for children.[27] Poverty matters because poor children are at least twice as likely as other children to suffer stunted growth or lead poisoning, or to be kept back in school. More than half of poor Americans (55 percent) experience serious deprivations during the year. This is defined as a lack of food, utility shutoffs, crowded or substandard housing, or lack of a stove or refrigerator. Poor households are more than 15 times as likely to experience hunger.[28]

The most often expressed dream of the children in the elementary school in the housing project was for safety. They wanted an end to violence, gangs, drive-by shootings, crime and drugs. However, an examination of the crime statistics for November, 2004 to March, 2005, showed a disparity in the numbers and types of crimes between the low-income 207 zip-code area around the housing project and elementary school and a much more affluent and exclusive 209 zip-code area of the city only five miles away.[29] Both areas report to the Central Substation of the San Antonio Police Department.

Table 9.1 San Antonio Police Department Central Substation Crimes (Nov.04-Mar.05)

Category of Crime	Total #	# in 207	207 % of Total	# in 209	209 % of Total
Vehicle Theft	286	77	27	6	2
Burglary Vehicle	965	277	28.7	44	4.6
Theft	1612	492	31	37	2.3
Burglary	733	304	41	38	5
Robbery	188	95	50.5	1	.5
Aggravated Assault	360	164	46	5	1.3
Forcible Rape	52	25	48	3	5.7

Homicide	7	5	71	0	0
Total	**4203**	**1439**	**34**	**134**	**3.2**

As listed on the department website, the definitions used by the San Antonio Police Department for categories used in the district crime lists are as follows:

Vehicle Theft: The theft or attempted theft of a motor vehicle, including the stealing of automobiles, trucks, busses, motorcycles, motor scooters, snowmobiles, etc.

Burglary Vehicle: Thefts from motor vehicles.

Theft: The unlawful taking, carrying, leading, or riding away of property from the possession of another. It includes such crimes a shoplifting, pocket-picking, purse-snatching, thefts of motor vehicle parts or accessories, bicycle thefts, etc., in which no use of force, violence, or fraud occurs.

Burglary: The unlawful entry of a structure to commit a felony or theft. The use of force is not required to classify an offense as burglary.

Robbery: The taking or attempt to take anything of value from the care, custody, or control of a person or persons by force or threat of force or violence and/or by putting the victim in fear.

Aggravated Assault: The unlawful attack by one person upon another for the purpose of inflicting severe or aggravated bodily injury. Aggravated assault is usually accompanied by the use of a weapon or by means likely to produce death or great bodily harm.

Forcible Rape: The carnal knowledge of a female forcibly and against her will. Attempts to commit rape by force or threat of force are also included; however, statutory rape (without force) and other sex offenses are excluded.

Homicide: The willful (non negligent) killing of one human being by another.

In comparing the types of crimes, it can be seen that the more violent types were much more likely to occur in the 207 area than in the 209 neighborhood. These crimes involve an attack on another person where there is great risk of or actual bodily injury to the victim, such as robbery, aggravated assaults, forcible rapes and homicides. There were 5 homicides in 207 and none in 209. These numbers are even more disparate. The 5 homicides in the 207 area represented 71 percent of *all* those reported in the Central Substation.

Children living with these high numbers of violent crimes cannot feel safe—not in their homes, not on the street, not in their school classrooms. When survival is difficult, learning must take a role of lesser importance.

Down the hall in the elementary school, the following anonymous poem was on a poster on the wall:

The world of tomorrow they say when it comes
Will free every city and town of its slums.
So if you like gardens where children can play

Let's make the world of tomorrow today.
The world of tomorrow will care for its youth
And teach them in all things to search for the truth.
So parents and children together let's say:
"Let's make the world of tomorrow TODAY!"

This beautiful sentiment is what is generally expressed in the dreams of the parents and children of this area. However, the reality is that the slums still exist and there are no gardens where children can play. Crime and danger are outside of every door of every home and every classroom. Society is not making the efforts necessary to bring about the *world of tomorrow*. So, the following anonymous poem posted on the wall in one of the classrooms seems to be more appropriate:

*Living on the Edge of Rage!
tolerance
accidental situations
flexibility
acceptance of circumstances
making best of things
handling anger
respect for others
need to learn

If the parents and children living in poverty can learn tolerance and flexibility, if they can accept their circumstances and make the best of things, perhaps they can become productive members of society. This does not mean giving up. It means growing. It means learning to control one's anger. It means striving to live harmoniously with others. It means becoming a citizen who is educated and has a voice that is exercised to cause change. Then and only then will all of them, and especially the children, have access to the beautiful "world of tomorrow."

Notes

1.   Edelman, M.W. (1989). In Andrews, Biggs, & Seidel (Eds.). *The Columbia world of quotations.* New York, NY: Columbia University Press. eNotes.com Retrieved 12/14/2006 from http://history.eNotes.com/famous-quotes/children-cannot-eat-rhetoric-and-they-cannot-be.
2.   Blair, G.R. (2005). *Helping your kids set goals.* Retrieved 6/5/04 from www.FamilyFirst.net/parenting/goalsguy.asp
3.   Ibid.
4.   Ibid.
5.   Ibid.
6.   Payne, R.K. (1998). *A Framework for understanding poverty (Revised edition).* Baytown, TX: RFT Publishing Co.
7.   Maslow, A.H. (1998). *Toward a psychology of being* (3rd Ed.). New York: John Wiley & Sons.

8. Heffner, C. (2002). Section 2, Maslow's hierarchy of needs; Chapter 10, Humanistic theory. *Personality synopsis.* Retrieved 4/18/05 from http://allpsych.com/personalitysynopsis/maslow.html

9. Maslow, A.H. (1998).

10. Ibid

11. Norwood, G. (2004). *Maslow's hierarchy of needs.* Retrieved 1/19/06 from http://www.deepermind.com/maslow.

12. Children's Defense Fund (2003a). *Children in Texas.* Washington, D.C. Retrieved 6/05/06 from http://www.childrensdefense.org/data/childreninthestates/tx.

13. Ibid.

14. Children's Defense Fund (2004b). *The road to dropping out, Minority students & academic factors correlated with failure to complete high school.* Washington, D.C. Retrieved 4/22/05 from http://www.childrensdefense.org.

15. Children's Defense Fund (2004a). *Educational resource disparities for minority and low-income children..* Washington, D.C. Retrieved 4/22/05 from http://www.childrensdefense.org.

16. Ibid., 1.

17. Haycock, K. (1998). Good teaching matters: How well-qualified teachers can close the gap. *Thinking K-16*, 3(2). Washington, D.C.: The Education Trust, 1-14.

18. National Research Council (2002). *Minority students in special and gifted education.* Washington, D.C.: National Academy Press, 174.

19. National Center for Education Statistics (2004). *The condition of education 2004.* Washington, DC: U.S. Department of Education, Institute of Education Sciences.

20. National Commission on Teaching and America's Future (2003). *No dream denied: A pledge to America's children*, 10. Washington, D.C.: Children's Defense Fund Press.

21. Texas Center for Educational Research (2000). *The cost of teacher turnover.* Austin, TX. Retrieved 6/3/06 from http://www.tcer.org/publications/teacher_turnover_full.doc

22. Children's Defense Fund (2004a).

23. National Center for Education Statistics.

24. National Research Council.

25. National Center for Education Statistics.

26. Children's Defense Fund (2003a).

27. Children's Defense Fund (2003b).

28. Children's Defense Fund (2003b).

29. San Antonio Police Department (2005). Retrieved 2/4/05 from http://www.sanantonio.gov/sapd/DATA/CENTDATA0105.htm

Chapter 10
Josie's Future—Where We Go From Here

Teachers are the guides, stimulators, energizers, and helpers. They hold the keys that unlock the storehouse of knowledge. . . . To take a child by the hand and help lead the child into the good life, while safeguarding and fostering his or her uniqueness, is an awesome task. Teachers need all the help they can get.
Dorothy Rubin[1]

The fate of empires depends upon the education of the youth.
Aristotle[2]

What do the years of research mean? What do all these figures and the mountains of statistics mean? What do they mean for society? What do they mean for leaders of our country, states and cities? What do they mean for individual citizens? What do they mean for educators? "[Homelessness]bodes poorly for the future of the city, as so many children must try to develop physically, mentally and intellectually without a permanent roof over their heads."[3] Kozol believes that society should be concerned about "the way that homelessness creates an underclass, enhances the underclass that may already have existed, and, combining newly poor and always-poor together in one common form of penury, assigns the children of them all to an imperiled life."[4] If this is the crisis we still face today, how do we make the changes necessary to give all the children like Josie and her brothers and sisters the chance at life they so desperately need and so genuinely deserve?

Homelessness is the result of a combination of *systemic factors* and *individual risk factors* which are much too complex for a single solution. Any strategies attempting to break the cycle of homelessness and/or prevent future homelessness must be based on an understanding of the root causes, the degrees of homelessness, and the factors that cause it to persist.[5] The *systemic factors* are conditions beyond a person's direct control that can cause and/or perpetuate homelessness. These include the lack of affordable housing, under-funded mental health and substance abuse treatment facilities, low-wage jobs, limited transportation, and an educational system that does not properly prepare people for the job market. The *individual risk factors* that lead to homelessness include substance abuse and addiction, mental illness, learning disabilities, low educational achievement, poor financial management, poor job skills, and/or poor job histories and extended reliance on public assistance.

The National Foundation Advisory Group for Ending Homelessness believes, "Addressing the systemic issues requires an emphasis on advocacy, policy, public education, and other efforts that work to effect change in the system."[6] Private corporations must work with charities to make public money go farther and tailor strategies to meet the specific needs of the homeless population. More and safer housing must be provided. Treatment centers, guidance, jobs and health care must all be coordinated and the services taken *to* those in need wherever they are. Then formerly homeless individuals must be integrated into the community so they are not stigmatized.

The Partnership for Hope identified community groups that must work together to meet these needs: Government, Citizens, Business Leaders, Philanthropists, Human Services Providers, the Religious Community, Urban Planners, Parents, and Educators.[7] Among the needs that must be met by these collective groups are: housing, human services, and education. However, if these needs are to be met, attitudes and beliefs of the public must be altered and society as a whole must see the homeless in a different light. In *Amazing Grace, The Lives of Children and the Conscience of a Nation,* Jonathan Kozol quoted Lawrence Mead, a professor of political science at New York University, from the May 19, 1992, *New York Times,* as saying "If poor people behaved rationally, they would seldom be poor for long in the first place."[8] Kozol continues, "Many social scientists today appear to hold this point of view and argue that the largest portion of the suffering poor people undergo has to be blamed upon their own 'behaviors', a word they tend to pluralize."[9] Kozol observes that ideas regarding the homeless are "divorced from any realistic context that includes the actual conditions of their lives. If we saw the people in these neighborhoods as part of the same human family to which we belong, we'd never put them in such places to begin with. But we do not think of them that way."[10]

Unfortunately, attitudes such as these still persist with much of the general public and a great many policymakers. Few seem to realize that the real *face* of homelessness is not that of the bum on the corner or under the bridge. The homeless include children laughing, playing, dreaming and hoping. It includes those who struggle in school and a few who excel. The *face* of homelessness is the face of Josie, her siblings, and all the other children like them. They are the helpless, hopeless victims we must reach and for whom we must work to change circumstances and improve the future.

What Society Must Do

In *A Plan, Not a Dream: How to End Homelessness in Ten Years,* the Board of

Directors of the National Alliance to End Homelessness state that ending homelessness is "within the nation's grasp."[11] They give four steps to end the cycle of homelessness in ten years. These steps were examined by the Mayor's Task Force, and adopted in January, 2005, by the City Council of San Antonio.[12] The steps are:

Step One: Plan for Outcomes

There must be a paradigm shift from *managing* homelessness to *eradicating* it. To do this, community groups must have information critically important for making the necessary decisions for meeting the needs of the homeless. "Basic needs: health care and education, become an afterthought when parents and children must first find shelter."[13] Therefore, there must be a plan for meeting those needs so that people can remain housed.

Step Two: Close the Front Door

Preventing homelessness or making speedy placement in housing is absolutely essential. "Prevention holds the promise of saving money."[14] Homeless *prevention* should use available resources for those *most likely* to become homeless. This includes families behind in their rent or facing eviction, those reentering general society from incarceration, young people outgrowing foster care, or women and children escaping domestic violence.[15] Keeping people from becoming homeless in the first place is easier and less expensive than moving them from the street or shelter into housing after they become homeless. "Policies to end homelessness must include jobs that pay livable wages. In order to work, families with children need access to quality child care that they can afford, and adequate transportation. Education and training are also essential elements in preparing parents for better paying jobs to support their families."[16] Providing these will go a long way toward helping prevent homelessness.

Step Three: Open the Back Door

Along with housing, people need an integrated array of social services. Community groups must coordinate access to social services so the cycle of homelessness can be broken. It is expensive and counterproductive for people to spend years in shelters or transitional housing. The National Foundation Advisory Group for Ending Homelessness found permanent supportive housing to be extremely successful and is "a solution that will save money as it reduces the use of other public systems."[17] They found it could save over $16,000 per household per year. Social services must also be available in convenient locations for ready access. These locations could include community centers, schools, clinics and so forth.

Step Four: Build the Infrastructure

No plan to end homelessness can succeed unless there is adequate affordable housing. The National Foundation Advisory Group for Ending Homelessness stated, "Community collaborations through a Continuum of Care and Ten Year Plans offer a variety of opportunities to provide support."[18] In January, 2005, San Antonio adopted a Ten Year Plan to End Chronic Homelessness and established a Continuum of Care to coordinate efforts across social agencies, support groups and government entities.

"The precipice on which many poor San Antonio families stand is growing more crowded all the time. For many poor families, a layoff, serious illness or other unforeseen occurrence could force them into even more unbearable living conditions, which may be evidenced by the rise in homelessness in San Antonio."[19] "The chilling fact, from any point of view, is that small children have become the fastest-growing sector of the homeless."[20] This fact has not changed in the nearly 20 years since Jonathan Kozol wrote those words!

There are several options for housing those experiencing homelessness. *Emergency shelters* provide a clean environment to sleep, humane care, some meals, and referrals to other agencies. The shelter operated by the San Antonio Metropolitan Ministries (SAMM) is one of approximately 15 emergency shelters in San Antonio. It is the site of much of this research and where Josie and her family lived periodically and for various lengths of time for over two years. On February 19, 2005, *The San Antonio Express News,* ran an advertisement for the SAAM shelter for their Third Annual Birdhouse Building Contest, an activity that raises money for the shelter. Statistics were given in that advertisement regarding the situation in the city:

> Today there are over 25,000 homeless individuals in San Antonio, and of that total, 38 percent are families. Within these families, 43 percent of the members are children. SAMMinistries assists an average of 500 individuals including 200 children every day of the year with shelter and services. Last year, the agency cared for nearly 4,500 individuals and provided almost 163,000 bed nights of shelter and services to the area's homeless.[21]

Transitional housing offers comprehensive services for up to two years to help people become self-sufficient. Josie and her siblings would truly have benefited from being placed in transitional housing and gaining some stability in their lives and continuity in their educational experiences. However, they were never qualified for such placement because of the actions of their mother. During the early part of this research, their mother met a man living in the shelter. They decided to leave and move, together with her children, into a very low-rent, substandard apartment. They remained there for about 8 months. Shortly after the birth of her fifth child, the mother left that man and moved back into the shelter with her children. They remained in the shelter for about 6 months. Josie and her school-aged siblings settled into the classroom at the elementary school, made friends, and began to make academic progress. The mother then met another man in the shelter and, again, moved her family out of the shelter to live with him. Within the year, she was back in the shelter, now with 6 children. She did not avail herself of any training or further her education. She could not obtain a job that would support her family and provide the necessary day-care for her children. Minimum wage jobs for which she was qualified simply would not adequately support all of them. She and her children seemed doomed to this vicious cycle because of bad choices she continued to make. She was not able to give her children the benefit of transitional housing and, eventually, public and more permanent housing. Josie and the other children continued to be victims of this physical and emotional upheaval.

Public housing is provided by agencies within the community. According to the Mayor's Task Force on Hunger and Homelessness, the San Antonio Housing Authority (SAHA) serves the housing needs of nearly 21,000 households.[22] SAHA owns and manages 6,350 public housing units, including 30 family housing developments, 31 senior housing developments, and the Section 8 Housing Voucher Program for over 12,000 households through privately owned rental property. These rental units are located in 61 developments throughout the city. As of August 1, 2005, the number of people on the waiting list for placement in a housing unit was 15,300.[23] The elementary school where portions of this research were conducted is located in one of the subsidized housing projects administered by SAHA. This is the elementary school attended by Josie, her siblings, and the other children from the shelter.

The National Foundation Advisory Group for Ending Homelessness has said, "If foundations join forces in local and national efforts, homelessness can be ended before it becomes a permanent feature of the national landscape."[24] It seems that the problem could be solved if our society *truly* desired to do so and worked toward that end. However, much of our society and many city governments have chosen to view the homeless more like Stuart Bykofsky, a columnist for *Newsweek Magazine*, who wrote, "There are people living on the streets of most American cities, turning sidewalks into dormitories. They are called the homeless. . . . Often they are called worse. They are American's living nightmare. . . . They have got to go."[25] Bykofsky continues, "I find it ironical that my tax money keeps the street—their home—paved and clean. That makes me their landlord. I want to evict them."[26] Society often views the homeless not as people who have certain human qualities, but as outcasts. When this is the view, pity grows into weariness; weariness becomes impatience; impatience turns into annoyance; and annoyance eventually develops into contempt. The homeless are beneath us, the problem lies with the homeless him/herself; and, as a society, we are not obligated to help in any way. This attitude must be changed if the problem is to be solved.

On November 30, 2006, the San Antonio City Council approved a plan for a near-downtown campus which will offer an array of social and practical services to help the homeless of the city get off the street and move toward self-sufficiency. The estimated cost for the program and facilities is $30 million and it is due to be functional by December 2008. The plan includes a 600-bed facility on 15 acres within 1.5 miles of downtown. There will be substance abuse and detoxification services, a medical center, a kitchen for resident and community meals, a day center, a chapel and green spaces. The idea behind this plan is to do more to treat the root causes of homelessness rather than to just provide temporary solutions. In his statement to the press regarding the Council decision, Mayor Hardberger said, "I continue to be thankful to live in a community represented by this council that has shown so much compassion." Community Initiatives Director, Dennis Campa, said, "Rather than using police, emergency rooms, courts and jails as a way to funnel the homeless into social services, having a one-stop shop for such services would be more cost-effective in the long run."[27]

What Individuals Can Do

The National Coalition for the Homeless has identified ways in which the general population and/or individual citizens can help end homelessness. People can volunteer by working at a shelter, helping to build or fix up houses or shelters, teaching professional skills or job training, sharing hobbies, taking the homeless to a community event, organizing an event at a shelter, or working with children. They can also become advocates for the homeless, helping create the systemic changes needed to end it.[28] Advocacy can take the form of connecting to a coalition, responding to legislative alerts, following local politics, educating community leaders, involving the media, registering homeless people to vote, sponsoring a Hunger and Homelessness Awareness Week, joining a national homeless rights organization, and becoming more aware of attitudes toward the homeless. We must "remind ourselves that people who are in such situations are still *people* first—just people who are going through a difficult period in their lives. In a time when they may find it difficult to hold onto their sense of humanity, it is particularly important that we do not use language that further diminishes the dignity of people in homeless situations."[29]

Another way in which individuals can help end homelessness is to contribute material assistance such as clothing, services, household goods, books, computers, survival kits, job opportunities, and support for a person or family. Other ways to contribute include raising funds for a program, giving directly to people experiencing homelessness, and, most importantly, smiling. "Whether or not you choose to give change, please don't look away from homeless people as if they do not exist. Making eye contact, saying a few words, or smiling can reaffirm the humanity of a person at a time when homelessness seems to have stripped it away. Most people will be glad simply to be acknowledged."[30] Lastly, to help in the eradication of homelessness, people must continue to educate themselves, their families and their community. Follow the local news, take advantage of teachable moments and talk to children about homelessness, read and talk to friends and acquaintances about the problem. "Opening up a dialogue is an essential first step we can all take in confronting this difficult problem."[31] Robert Slavin explains, "[W]e cannot have a just or peaceful society if major segments of it see little hope for their children. . . . [W]e need to move away from seeing children as being at risk towards seeing them as being at promise."[32] This takes discussion, consideration, and changes in attitude and perception.

While many needs must be met by cooperation and coordination of many agencies, the need for education must be met by the educational system, schools, and, ultimately, the teachers who have homeless children in their classrooms on a day-to-day basis. "Homelessness is not a housing issue; it is an education issue, a children's issue, and a family issue."[33]

> [B]eing homeless means more than not having a place to sleep. Being homeless means having no place to save the things that connect you to your past, losing all contact with friends and family, uprooting your children from school. It means suffering the frustration and degradation of living hand to mouth, depending on the generosity of strangers or the efficiency of a government agency for your survival, for your children's survival[34]

This is the reality that has the most profound impact on children and this is the situation that must be addressed by schools and teachers.

What Schools Must Do

School has become the only agency that deals with every child, every day. Thus, the school must serve as the center of advocacy for children. Research identified actions that schools must take to be effective in dealing with children from extreme poverty and/or homelessness. These are: heightened awareness of the problem, collaboration and coordination of services, proper school and classroom placement, access to the necessary school supplies, transportation to and from school, and tutoring and mentoring to improve achievement.[35]

> Schools do not have the power to change the home conditions of students, but we must recognize that terms such as "disadvantaged," "deprived," and "at risk" are convenient labels that allow the schools to accept failure and to avoid responsibility for meeting the needs of all students.[36]

"Early childhood education lays the foundation for future academic success; it encourages a child's cognitive and social development in the short-term and produces substantial educational benefits in the long-term."[37] Schools should offer preschool children a head start on their education by providing effective programs with activities designed to enhance mental and social development and the behaviors and attitudes for success in school. Starting early with children can help level the playing field as they move into elementary school so that they may be academically prepared to move forward in their education as well as compete with others in their learning.[38]

There is a moral imperative for educators to reach out to homeless children and youths. Public schools must serve the most disenfranchised. However, one of the challenges facing educators trying to meet the educational needs of these children is that the school system was not designed to serve such a mobile and specialized population. The public educational system was designed to serve mainstream or *average* families.

For schools to meet the challenges posed by homeless children, changes must be made to operating procedures. We cannot expect the lives of the students to change in order to make it easier to run the schools.[39] Schools must review and revise policies, practices, and procedures to remove barriers to access and success in school for homeless children and youths. The McKinney-Vento Act was enacted as an effort to do just that. It was designed to remove barriers so that children could remain in their local school if they became homeless and moved onto the street or into a shelter. The act states that students are to remain in the school they were attending *when* they became homeless. The intent is to prevent children from having to change schools and lose valuable teaching/learning time and face the social adjustment caused by mobility. However, the *intent* of the law must be enforced, not the *letter* of the law. In one San Antonio school, a second grade girl, new to the school at the beginning of the school year, was assigned to a classroom where the teacher and a student teacher worked very diligently to make the child feel at home and a part of the class. After approximately six weeks, the girl finally had made friends, felt comfortable in the classroom and had begun to make academic progress. At that time, the central office staff discovered this child had attended another area school the previous year and had become homeless over the summer months. Because of the strict interpretation of the McKinney-Vento Act, it was determined that she should return to her previous school. As the child was taken from her current classroom and school, she was heard screaming, crying and begging to stay in the school that she now considered *her* school. This is an injustice and a misinterpretation of the requirements of the law. This is where we must enforce the *spirit* and the *intent* of the law. "School is one of the few stable, secure places in the lives of homeless children and youth—a place where they can acquire the skills needed to help them escape poverty."[40]

Schools must coordinate and collaborate with shelters and other homeless service providers to help ensure that homeless children and youths have prompt and convenient access to social services. Many communities now have social service providers and agents in their schools for easy access by both students and parents. This can ease the burden for transportation to those services and can provide additional contact for those in need of them.

Schools and communities must provide supplemental educational programs, such as before- and after-school, weekend, holiday, and summer programs, for homeless children and youths. Helping them to become successful in school and career training is vital to the reduction of truancy and delinquency, and, ultimately, to the eradication of homelessness. The goal of any school should be to guide *all* students into becoming productive and contributing members of society.

School districts now have homeless liaisons whose responsibilities include: providing outreach in areas where homeless children live, establishing collaborations to connect families with available services, and working closely with families to expedite enrollment, assessment, and referrals in school. This position is vital to making those who are homeless comfortable and to providing for their specialized and specific needs.

Schools must also ensure that children and youths have access to the materials and supplies, including school supplies, clothes, and hygiene products, necessary for attendance and success in school. Providing the necessities is vitally important for children in extreme poverty because, if the school does not provide for them, they must do without. Children with more resources available to them from home and family have ready access to things not supplied by the school.

Transportation must be provided to homeless children when shelters or living arrangements are in dangerous environments or when children would otherwise be unable to attend school. This is even necessary when the child lives close to school. However, as Mordecai Green said in *The Street Lawyer*, "Governments are balancing budgets on the backs of the poor."[41] Therefore, transportation is often one of the barriers that is the most difficult to overcome because of the costs to the school districts and cities. There is also the complicating factor of the logistics of getting each child to the proper school regardless of where he/she is currently residing. This adds to the cost of providing proper placement for each child.

Kozol, said, "Teachers speak of kids who fall into a deep sleep at their desks because conditions in their [shelter] denied them a night's rest. How much can such children learn?"[42] Unfortunately, homeless children are too young to have a voice or vote and their parents have no lobbyists in Washington or in City Hall. "[T]he homeless have no voice. No one listens, no one cares, and they expect no one to help them. So when they try to use the phone to get benefits due them, they get nowhere. They are put on hold, permanently. Their calls are never returned. They have no addresses. The bureaucrats don't care, and so they screw the very people they're supposed to help."[43] This must be changed and schools must take the lead in making the difference for these children. Schools and agencies serving these children and their families must work collaboratively to coordinate efforts.

Schools with high proportions of low-income children have higher numbers of inexperienced teachers, fewer computers, less Internet access, and larger class sizes than schools with lower proportions of low-income children.[44] Thus, the children who stand to gain the most from quality schools often do not have access to them. Federal, state, and local policies that promote more equitable distribution of funding and resources across school districts could resolve such discrepancies. Inequities in funding cause inequities in facilities for schools. "There is something wrong with a society where money is available to do . . . research but not to remove lead poison from the homes and schools of children."[45] It is a matter of societal priorities. "[F]or children in poverty, succeeding in school is a matter of life and death. They cannot be rock stars or players in the NBA. They must make it in school or spend their lives in hopelessness and desperation. Children in poverty have no family resources or networks to help them start careers or businesses; they must succeed in school to have any hope of occupational mobility."[46] Hart-Shegos believes that "[t]he effects of homelessness can be minimized—maybe even reversed." She says that "[w]hile research on homeless children paints an overwhelmingly bleak picture of their current and future status, there is hope that with early and consistent intervention strategies, children can learn to overcome many of the detrimental effects of their poverty and homeless experiences."[47] The strategies she suggests are: access to services, housing, parenting support, after school programs, assessment and monitoring of children's development, and assisting children and parents in participating in school activities. These interventions would give children who have been homeless a chance to build the resiliency and competence they need to break the detrimental cycle of homelessness.

For children to build this resilience and competence, we must provide the neediest students with the very best teachers. "[M]uch of what we have blamed on children and their families for decades is actually the result of things we have done to them. As a nation, we have deprived our neediest students of the very ingredient most important to learning: a highly qualified teacher."[48] What must be done so that children in extreme poverty get the best instruction from the best teachers?

What Teachers Must Do

"For the children and youths in poverty from diverse cultural backgrounds, . . . having effective teachers is a matter of life and death. These children have no life options for achieving decent lives other than by experiencing success in school. For them, the stakes involved in schooling are extremely high."[49] "If we only took the simple step of assuring that poor and minority children had highly qualified teachers, about half of the achievement gap would disappear. If we went further and assigned our best teachers to the students who most need them, . . . there's persuasive evidence to suggest that we could entirely close the gap."[50]

However, "[a]dvocates for children . . . speak about the many elementary schools and junior high schools in which students seldom see a certified teacher but are instructed, for the most part, by 'provisionals,' or permanent subs, while more experienced teachers are assigned to schools in less abandoned neighborhoods. . . . The over-crowding of children in these schools compounds the chaos caused by staffing difficulties."[51] The No Child Left Behind Legislation and its provision that all teachers be *highly qualified* is an attempt to provide the best teachers for all students.[52]

Research has identified what teachers must know and do to be effective in dealing with homeless children.[53] These teachers must have a desire and dedication to work with this specialized population along with a sensitivity to their problems. They must have strategies for teaching and the materials necessary to meet the needs of each of these students.

To understand the mind of the poor . . . child, we need to listen to people from such backgrounds rather than to expert psychologists or educators. They are the ones who can help us understand what should constitute the curriculum for such students, how to make up for the deficiencies in their home background, how to understand the value of their own superior skills and to measure them by that. Many among us educators are . . . exposed only to the world of books . . . ignorant of the richness of the mass culture and . . . blind to our students' needs and problems.[54]

Teachers must be sensitive and skilled at working with students from diverse cultures. They must help students use what they already know to be successful in the classroom and in the world. Failure on the part of teachers, schools and society to do this will only perpetuate the problem of homelessness. It must be recognized that education, training and skills are less expensive and more easily provided than social services and assistance to those who are unable to be contributing members of society.

In *Star Teachers of Children in Poverty*, Martin Haberman examined the attitudes, philosophies, behaviors and teaching styles of teachers who are successful in dealing with children living in extreme poverty. He calls these effective and successful teachers *stars*.[55] He states, "Star teachers conceive that their primary goal is turning kids on to learning—i.e., engaging them in becoming independent learners."[56] "They persist until their students also see learning as sufficient reason for being in school."[57] Teachers cannot give up on students for whom learning is difficult even though it may make it hard to run the school. "But if we lose them, school is no longer school. It is a hospital which tends to the healthy and rejects the sick."[58]

One of the most important issues for excellent teachers of children in poverty is creating a safe learning environment. They must "create safe havens where, for a good part of every day, the madness of violence will not intrude and their children will experience freedom from fear."[59]

[P]oor and minority children depend on their teachers like no others. In the hands of our best teachers, the effects of poverty and institutional racism melt away, allowing these students to soar to the same heights as young Americans from more advantaged homes. . . . [Nothing should] deter us from doing what it takes to assure that poor and minority youngsters get at least their fair share of effective, well-prepared teachers.[60]

Long-term relationships between teachers and students can be created by "[k]eeping students with the same teacher(s) for two or more years."[61] The powerful message from poor students to all teachers is, "I'd have you paid by piecework. So much for each child who learns one subject. . . . Then . . . you would fight for the child who needs you most . . . you would wake up at night thinking about him and would try to invent new ways to teach him—ways that would fit his needs."[62]

Haberman found that star teachers were not overly concerned with classroom discipline. They "spend so little time on discipline because they have invested their time and effort creating learning activities that have helped them build caring relationships with each of the children."[63] "Many of the behaviors that students bring to school are necessary to help them survive outside of school....If students from poverty don't know how to fight physically, they are going to be in danger on the streets. But if that is their only method of resolving a problem, then they cannot be successful in school."[64] Payne says that any effective discipline program must move students toward self-control. This is done through the structure of the classroom and by guiding students to make appropriate and thoughtful choices.[65] Teachers must be sensitive and understand that the poorest child is, in essence, saying, "Every people has its own culture, and no people has less than the others. Our culture is a gift that we bring to you. A vital breath of air to relieve the dryness of your books written by men who have done nothing but read books."[66] A caring responsive learning community is essential for every child, but especially for the neediest ones.[67]

Haberman found that star teachers do not assign homework in the traditional sense. "They try to create assignments that youngsters are able to do independently and successfully. . . . Often, such homework assignments place the child in the position of expert or explainer to—rather than someone in need of help from – a parent. This means that homework is carefully conceived and not simply assigned."[68] To connect with their students and the parents, excellent teachers strive to learn about their students' lives. In aiming to make learning more meaningful and relevant, they use the information about their students to make specific connections between a particular learning activity and something that will mark it as meaningful for the individual student. They strive to deepen "the bonds of mutual respect between themselves and the children."[69] In other words, they "[p]ut students ahead of subject matter. . . . [and] [n]ever go through the meaningless motion of "covering" material apart from students' involvement and learning."[70] These teachers see that everything connected with school must be meaningful to the lives of their students if those students are to gain the educational benefit for which the activity was designed. Excellent teachers do not have students who would say, "Your text book covers all the world but never mentions hunger, monopolies, political systems or racialism. Nothing is found in the newspaper that could help us pass your exams."[71]

Teachers must also teach coping strategies and must directly teach classroom survival skills. These make a difference in achievement, success and self-esteem for each student. Payne states,

> Requiring daily goal-setting and procedural self-talk would move many of these students light years ahead. In the beginning, goal-setting would focus on what a student wants to accomplish by the end of each day and by the end of the week. Goals would be in writing. At the end of the day, five minutes would need to be taken with the class to see if the goals were met or not. Procedural self-talk would begin in the written form [and must be] tied to a specific task.[72]

Low student-teacher ratios with a high degree of individualization are critically important so that the needs of each child can be addressed. Only then can we insure the future success of these children. "The [ideal] model stresses the teaching of concepts, analysis and problem-solving to instill and strengthen reading, writing, science and mathematics skills, and discourages the use of repetition and drills."[73] These students must learn the skills and have the knowledge necessary for coping with life in the real world. With these skills and knowledge, they will be able to get jobs, make a living, raise families, and become productive citizens. Without them, they may be doomed to the vicious cycle of homelessness.

Star teachers "do not blame parents. . . . Effective teachers continue to believe that most parents care a great deal and, if approached in terms of what they can do, will be active, cooperative partners."[74] Helping parents know how to assist and support their children is vital.

What We All Must Do

After several years, I lost track of Josie and her family. I often think about them and wonder what became of them. I truly cared about her and all the other children I met at the SAMM shelter. The last I knew of the family, the mother had met yet another man in the shelter and they had moved out together. Josie had lost her spark and was not longer the vivacious, eager student I had first met. Jessie, her brother, had become involved with a gang, was in an alternative school, not doing well, and had the very real potential of going to juvenile detention or even more severe incarceration. Eva, Josie's oldest sister, had dropped out of school during her eighth grade year and taken up life on the street, was doing drugs, and was supporting herself and her habit through prostitution. Angela, the middle sister, who had excelled in school, had begun to falter in her grades, lose interest, and seemed doomed to follow Eva's example. I worry that I did not do enough to change their trajectory in life so they could break free of the hold homelessness had on them. A part of me feels that I failed Josie and the others. Perhaps if I had known all I know now about the subject of homelessness, I could have done more. The one thing I do know is that I am better equipped today to help other children and will continue to spread the word so that other individuals and social action groups become equipped to help as well. I also make sure that the preservice teachers I work with are sensitive to the problems and have the skills and knowledge to work effectively with these children. Perhaps this is the most powerful tool I have to make a difference in the lives of homeless children and those who may become homeless in the future.

By allowing homeless children to grow up without a focus on education, society not only fails to cultivate a future for these children, but also promotes a continued cycle of poverty. . . . By prioritizing the education of society's most vulnerable children, we invest in the nation's social infrastructure. . . . [T]he magnitude of the challenge is great. However, the potential of the homeless children who are inspired to adopt education as a way of life is even greater.[75]

As individuals and as a society, we must begin to look at the homeless with a different attitude and understanding. We must see them as members of *our* society, fellow human beings. We must know that they have potential. We must realize that they need our help to reach that potential. We must reach out, especially to the children. We must *really see* the Josies, Evas, Angelas, Jessies, Rauls, Angels, and all the others. We must save them!

Robert Fulghum said it best.

[T]he lessons of kindergarten are hard to practice if they don't apply to you,. It's hard to share everything and play fair if you don't have anything to share and life is itself unjust. I think of the children of this earth who see the world through barbed wire, who live in a filthy rubbled mess not of their own making and that they can never clean up. They do not wash their hands before they eat. There is no water. Or soap. And some do not have hands to wash. They do not know about warm cookies and cold milk, only stale scraps and hunger. They have no blankie to wrap themselves in, and do not take naps because it is too dangerous to close their eyes.

Theirs is not the kindergarten of finger paint and nursery rhymes, but an X-rated school of harsh dailiness. Their teachers are not sweet women who care, but the indifferent instructors called Pain, Fear, and Misery. Like all children everywhere, they tell stories of monsters. Theirs are for real—what they have seen with their own eyes. In broad daylight. We do not want to know what they have learned.

But we know.

And it ain't kindergarten stuff.

The line between good and evil, hope and despair, does not divide the world between "us" and "them." It runs down the middle of every one of us.

I do not want to talk about what you understand about this world. I want to know what you will *do* about it. I do not want to know what you *hope*. I want to know what you will *work for*. I do not want your sympathy for the needs of humanity. I want your muscle. As the wagon driver said when they came to a long, hard hill, "Them that's going on with us, get out and push. Them that ain't, get out of the way."[76]

Notes

1.   Rubin, D. (2000). *Teaching elementary language arts: A balanced approach* (6th Ed.). Boston, MA: Allyn and Bacon. xxv.

2.   Aristotle (unknown) quoted on http://www.freerepublic.com/forum/A39eca0906518.htm.

3.   Partnership for Hope (1991). *Pride and Poverty, A Report on San Antonio.* San Antonio, TX. 102.

4.   Kozol, J. (1988) *Rachel and her children; Homeless families in America,* Crown Publishers, Inc., New York, NY. 20.

5.   Mayor's Task Force on Hunger and Homelessness (2005). *Ten-year plan to end*

chronic homelessness. San Antonio, TX.

6.   National Foundation Advisory Group for Ending Homelessness (2000). *Ending homelessness: The philanthropic role.* Washington, DC.: Neighborhood Funders Group. 7.

7.   Partnership for Hope.

8.   Kozol, J. (1995). *Amazing grace: The lives of children and the conscience of a nation*; Crown Publishers, Inc., New York, NY. 21.

Mead, L. (1992). *New York Times.* May 19, 1992.

9.   Kozol (1995). 21.

10.   Ibid., 181.

11.   National Alliance to End Homelessness (2000). *A plan: Not a dream, How to end homelessness in ten years.* Washington, DC. 1.

12.   Mayor's Task Force on Hunger and Homelessness.

13.   Partnership for Hope, 101.

14.   National Alliance to End Homelessness, 2.

15.   The National Foundation Advisory Group for Ending Homelessness.

16.   National Coalition for the Homeless (2001). *Homeless families with children.* Retrieved March 10, 2004 from http://www.nationalhomeless.org/families.html. 4.

17.   National Foundation Advisory Group for Ending Homelessness, 2.

18.   Ibid., 12.

19.   The Partnership for Hope, 102.

20.   Kozol (1988) 4.

21.   *San Antonio Express News* (February 19, 2005). San Antonio, TX. 4D.

22.   Mayor's Task Force on Hunger and Homelessness.

23.   SAHA (2006). San Antonio Housing Authority information website. Retrieved on 10/27/2006 from http://www.saha.org/public%20housing/html/public_housing.html.

24.   National Foundation Advisory Group for Ending Homelessness, 3.

25.   Bykofsky, S.D. (December 1, 1986). *Newsweek Magazine,* 12.

26.   Ibid., 13.

27.   Jesse, L.E. (2006). City takes step toward new way to aid homeless. *Express News,*   November   30,   2006.   retrieved   12/11/2006   from http://www.mysanantonio.com/news/citycouncil/stories/MYSA12106.01A.HomelessPlan

28.   National Coalition for the Homeless (2006b). *How YOU can help end homelessness: NCH Fact Sheet #19.* Washington, DC. Downloaded 10/31/2006 from http://www.nationalhomeless.org/publications/facts/you.pdf.

29.   Ibid., 4.

30.   Ibid., 6.

31.   Ibid., 7.

32.   Slavin, R.E. (1998). Can education reduce social inequity?. *Educational leadership,* 8.

33.   Institute for Children in Poverty (1999). Access to success: Meeting the educational needs of homeless children and families. New York, NY. 1.

34.   National Coalition for the Homeless (1989). *Homelessness in America: A summary.* New York, NY. 1.

35.   James, B.; Lopez, P.; Murdock, B.; Rouse, J.; & Walker, N. (1997). *Pieces of the puzzle.* Austin, TX: STAR (Support for Texas Academic Renewal) Center.

36.   Hartle-Schutte, D. (1993). Literacy development in Navajo homes: Does it lead to success in school?. *Language Arts,* 70(8), 650.

37.   Institute for Children and Poverty (1999). 1.

38.   Irish, K.; Schumacher, R.; and Lombardi, J. (2003). *Head start comprehensive*

services: A key support for early learning. Washington, DC: Center for Law and Social Policy.

39. James, Lopez, Murdock, Rouse & Walker

40. National Coalition for the Homeless (2006a). *Education of homeless children and youth: NCH Fact Sheet #10.* Washington, DC. Retrieved 7/14/2006 from http://www.nationalhomeless.org/publications/education.pdf. 3.

41. Grisham , J. (1999). *The street lawyer.* New York, NY: Island Books, Published by Dell Publishing a division of Random House, Inc. 202.

42. Kozol (1988). 86-87.

43. Grisham, 104.

44. Mayer, D.P.; Mullens, J.E.; & Moore, M.T. (2000). *Monitoring school quality: An indicators report* (NCES 2001-030). Washington, DC: US Department of Education, National Center for Education Statistics.

45. Kozol, J. (1995). 156.

46. Haberman, M. (1995). *Star teachers of children in poverty.* West Lafayette, IN: Kappa Delta Pi International Honor Society in Education. 40.

47. Hart-Shegos, E. (1999). *Homelessness and its effects on children.* Minneapolis, MN: Family Housing Fund. 6.

48. Haycock, K. (1998). Good teaching matters: How well-qualified teachers can close the gap. *Thinking K-16,* 3(2). Washington, D.C.: The Education Trust, 10.

49. Haberman, 1.

50. Haycock, 2.

51. Kozol (1995), 155.

52. No Child Left Behind (2004). United States Government. Retrieved 8/15/06 from www.ed.gov/nclb/methods/teachers/hqtflexibility.html.

53. James, Lopez, Murdock, Rouse & Walker .

54. Chithprabha, K. (2005). Letter to a teacher by schoolboys of Barbiana: A forgotten treatise on school education. *Thinking classroom, 6(2).* Newark, DE: International Reading Association. 34-35.

55. Haberman.

56. Ibid., 15.

57. Ibid., 18.

58. Chithprabha, 33.

59. Haberman, 91.

60. Haycock. 11, 13.

61. Payne, R.K. (1998). *A Framework for understanding poverty (Revised edition).* Baytown, TX: RFT Publishing Co. 95.

62. Chithprabha, 35.

63. Haberman, 4.

64. Payne, 100.

65. Ibid.

66. Chithprabha, 30.

67. Johnston, P.H. & Quinlan, M.E. (2002). A caring, responsible learning community. In Allington & Johnston (Eds.), R*eading to learn: Lessons from exemplary fourth-grade classrooms.* New York, NY: Guilford. 123-139.

68. Haberman, 10.

69. Ibid., 53.

70. Ibid., 90.

71. Chithprabha, 32.

72. Payne, 96.

73. Institute for Children and Poverty, 3.

74. Haberman, 11-12.

75. Institute for Children and Poverty, 5.

76. Fulghum, R. (1988). *It was on fire when I lay down on it*. New York, NY: Ivy Books. 106-107. Copyright © 1988, 1989 by Robert Fulghum. Used by permission of Villard Books, a division of Random House, Inc.

Resources

The following resources have been collected for readers to continue their study and gain more understanding regarding the problems and possible solutions to the critical issue of homelessness.

Books

Homeless Children

Ayer, E.H. (1997). *Homeless children (Overview)*. San Diego, CA: Lucient Books.

Berck, J. (1992). *No place to be: Voices of homeless children*. Boston, MA: Houghton Mifflin Company.

Boxill, N.A. (1990). *Homeless children: The watchers & the waiters*. New York, NY: Haworth Press.

Cwayna, K. (1993). *Knowing where the fountains are: Stories and stark realities of homeless youth*. Minneapolis, MN: Deaconess Press.

Flohr, J.K. (1998). *Transitional programs for homeless women with children: Education, employment training, and support services (Children of Poverty)*. New York, NY: Routledge.

Hertensten, J. (Ed.) (1995). *Home is where we live: Life at a shelter through a young girl's eyes.* Chicago, IL: Cornerstone Press Chicago.

Hubbard, J. (1991*). Shooting back: A photographic view of life by homeless children*. San Francisco, CA: Chronicle Books.

Kennedy, M. (2006). *Without a net: Middle class and homeless (with kids) in America*. New York, NY: Penguin Books.

Kozol, J. (1995*). Amazing grace: The lives of children and the conscience of a nation*. New York, NY: Crown Publishers.

Kozol, J. (1988*). Rachel and her children: Homeless families in America*. New York, NY: Crown Publishers.

Kryder-coe, J.H. (1991). *Homeless children & youth: A new American dilemma*. New Brunswick, NJ: Transaction Publishers.

Shane, P.G. (1996). *Sage sourcebooks for the human services #32: What about America's homeless children?: Hide and seek*. Thousand Oaks, CA: Sage Publication.

Vissing, Y.M. (1996). *Out of sight, out of mind: Homeless children and families in small-town America*. Lexington, KY: University Press of Kentucky.

Vostainis, P. (1999). *Homeless children: Problems and needs*. London, England: Jessica Kingsley Publishers.

Wallace, J., Finland, G. & Chalofsky, M. (1992). *Changing places: A kids view of shelter living*. Mt. Ranier, MD: Gryphon House.

Education and Training

Haberman, M. (1995). *Star teachers of children in poverty*. West Lafayette, IN: Kappa Delta Pi International Honor Society in Education.

Kozol, J. (1985*). Illiterate America*. Garden City, NY: Anchor Press/Doubleday.

Kozol, J. (1991). *Savage inequalities: Children in America's schools*. New York, NY: Crown Publishers.

Newman, R. (2001). *Educating homeless children: Witness to a cataclysm (children of poverty)*. New York, NY: Garland Publishing.

Quint, S. (1994). *Schooling homeless children: A working model for America's public schools*. New York, NY: Teachers College Press, Teachers College, Columbia University.

Payne, R.K. (1998). *A framework for understanding poverty (Revised edition)*. Baytown, TX: RFT Publishing Co.

Percy, M.S. (1997). *Not just a shelter kid: How homeless children find solace (Children of poverty)*. New York, NY: Routledge Press.

Rose, M. (1989). *Lives on the boundary*. New York, NY: Penguin Books.

Stronge, J.H. (1992). *Educating homeless children and adolescents: Evaluating policy and practice*. Newbury Park, CA: Sage Publications.

Taylor, D. & Dorsey-Gaines, C. (1988). *Growing up literate: Learning from inner-city families*. Portsmouth, NH: Heinemann.

Problems and Issues

Baumohl, J. (Ed) (1996). *Homelessness in America*. Phoenix, Arizona: Oryx Press.

Benge, L. (2004). *It's a God thing: True stories from a homeless shelter*. New York, NY: Tate Publishing.

Blau, J. (1992). *The visible poor: Homelessness in the United States*. New York, NY: Oxford University Press.

Borchard, K. (2005). *The word on the street: Homeless men in Las Vegas*. Las Vegas, NV: University of Nevada Press.

Burt, M.R. (1992). *Over the edge: The growth of homelessness in the 1980s*. New York, NY: Russell Sage Foundation.

Burt, M.R. & Cohen, B.E. (1989). *America's homeless: Numbers, characteristics, and programs that serve them*. Washington, DC: Urban Institute Press; Lanham, MD:

Distributed by University Press of America.

Coates, R.C. (1990). *A street is not a home: Solving America's homeless dilemma.* Buffalo, NY: Prometheus Books.

Connolly, D.R. (2000). *Homeless mothers: Face to face with women and poverty.* Minneapolis/St. Paul, MN: University of Minnesota Press.

DaCosta Nunez, R. (1996). *The new poverty: Homeless families in America.* New York, NY: Insight Books.

Desjarlais, R. (1997). *Shelter blues: Sanity and selfhood among the homeless (Contemporary ethnography).* Philadelphia, PA: University of Pennsylvania Press.

Doherty, J. (1999). *Services for homeless people.* Bristol, England: Policy Press.

Evans, M.A. (1988). *Homeless in America.* Washington, DC: Acropolis Books., Inc.

Greenhaven Press Staff (1995). *Homeless: Opposing viewpoints (96 Ed).* San Diego, CA: Greenhaven Press.

Gunning, M. (2004). *A shelter in our car.* San Francisco, CA: Children's Book Press (CA).

Harrington, M. (1981). *The other America: Poverty in the United States.* New York, NY: Penguin Books.

Harrington, M. (1984). *The new American poverty.* New York, NY: Holt, Rinehart, & Winston.

Kraljic, M.A. (Ed) (1992). *The homeless problem.* The reference shelf, 64(2). New York, NY: The H.W. Wilson Company.

Lyon-callo, V. (2004). *Inequality, poverty, and neoliberal governance: Activist ethnography in the homeless sheltering industry.* New York, NY: Broadway Press.

Rosen, M.J. (1992). *Home: A collaboration of authors & illustrators to aid the homeless.* New York, NY: Harper Collins Publishers.

Rossi, P.H. (1989). *Down and out in America: The origins of homelessness.* Chicago, IL: University of Chicago Press.

Rousseau, A.M. (1981). *Shopping bag ladies: Homeless women speak about their lives.* New York, NY: The Pilgrim Press.

Seltser, B.J. (1993). *Homeless families: The struggle for dignity.* Urbana, IL: University of Illinois Press.

Snow, D.A. & Anderson, L. (1993). *Down on their luck: A study of homeless street people.* Los Angeles, CA: University of California Press.

Solomon, C. & Jackson-Jobe, P. (1992*). Helping homeless people: Unique challenges and solutions.* Alexandria, VA: American Counseling Association.

Testa, M. (1996). *Someplace to go.* Morton Grove, IL: Albert Whitman & Company.

Timmer, D.A. (1994). *Paths to homelessness: Extreme poverty and the urban housing crisis.* Boulder, CO: Westview Press.

VanderStaay, S. (1992). *Street lives: An oral history of homeless Americans.* Philadelphia, PA: New Society Publishers.

Williams, M.E. (Ed.) (2004). *Poverty and the homeless (Current controversies).* San Diego, CA: Greenhaven Press.

Wilson, W.J. (1987). *The truly disadvantaged: The inner city, the underclass, and public policy.* Chicago, IL: University of Chicago Press.

Wilson, W.J. (1996). *When work disappears: The world of the new urban poor.* New York, NY: Knopf: Distributed by Random House.

Wright, J.D. (1987). *Homelessness and health.* Washington, DC: McGraw-Hill's Healthcare Information Center.

Wright, J.D. (1989). *Address unknown: The homeless in America.* Hawthorne, NY: Aldine de Gruyter Publishing Co.

Sociological Understanding

Bard, M. (1990). *Shadow women: Homeless women's survival stories.* Kansas City, MO: Sheed & Ward.

Choi, N.G. (1999). *Homeless families with children: A subjective experience of homelessness.* New York, NY: Springer Publishing Company.

Daly, G. (1996). *Homeless: Policies, strategies, and lives on the street.* New York, NY: Routledge.

Deollos, I.Y. (1997). *On becoming homeless: The shelterization process for homeless families.* Lanham, MD: University Press of America.

Dordick, G.A. (1997). *Something left to lose: Personal relations and survival among New York's homeless.* Philadelphia, PA: Temple University Press.

Ferrill, L. (1991). *Far cry from home: Life in a shelter for homeless women.* Chicago, IL: Noble Press.

Ferrell, F. (1985). *Trevor's place: The story of the boy who brings hope to the homeless.* San Francisco, CA: Harper & Row.

Fitzpatrick, S. (2000). *Young homeless people.* New York, NY: Palgrave MacMillan, Ltd.

Gerson, J. (2006). *Hope springs maternal: Homeless mothers talk about making sense of adversity.* New York, NY: Richard Altschuler & Associates, Inc.

Hughes, L.V. (2004). *Our homeless deserve better! A plea to all caring communities, because all homeless persons are somebody's relative.* Columbia, MD: Reval Publishing.

Jencks, C. (1994). *The homeless.* Boston, MA: Harvard University Press.

Marcus, A. (2005). *Where have all the homeless gone?* New York, NY: Berghahn Books, Inc.

Pugh, D. (1997). *I have arrived before my words: the autobiographical writings of homeless women.* Alexandria, VA: Charles River Press.

Rosenthal, R. (1994). *Homeless in paradise: A map of the terrain.* Philadelphia, PA: Temple University Press.

White, R.W. (1992). *Rude awakenings: What the homeless crisis tells us.* San Francisco, CA: ICS Press.

Williams, J.C. (2003). *A roof over my head: Homeless women and the shelter industry.* Boulder, CO: University Press of Colorado.

Literature – Fiction and Non-Fiction

Adult

Erlbaum, J. (2006). *Runaway: Homeless and alone on the streets of New York.* London, England: Ebury Press.

Gordon, R.J. (2003). *Sammy's red shirt: Lost boy, homeless girl.* New York, NY: Authorhouse.

Grisham, J. (1999). *The street lawyer.* New York, NY: Island Books, Published by Dell Publishing a division of Random House, Inc.

Hill, J. (1991). *You haven't to deserve: A gift to the homeless: Fiction.* Atlanta, GA: Task Force for the Homeless.

Hooks, U.B. Jr. (2006). *Guardian angels along my homeless path.* Bloomington, IN: Authorhouse.

Peterson, F.B. and King, V.E. (2003). *Gifts in the storm: A homeless man's Christmas story with CD.* New York, NY: Unicorn Publishing House.

Santoyo, R. (2005). *I love you, baby, I love you: Stories of homeless people in a border town.* New York, NY: PublishAmerica.

Woods, D.J. (2005). *Love and charity: The life and story of Louise Hunter and the Love and Charity Homeless Shelter.* New York, NY: PublishAmerica.

Redhed, A. (2005). *Murder and underwear: Working with the homeless in Chicago.* New York, NY: iUniverse, Inc.

Children

Bunting, E. (1991). *Fly away home.* New York, NY: Clarion Books.

DiSalvo-Ryan, D. (1991). *Uncle Willie and the soup kitchen.* New York, NY: Mulberry Books.

Haverfield, M. (2005). *Harriett the homeless raccoon.* Abilene, TX: Bright Sky Press.

Kid's Livin Life (2001). *The homeless hibernating bear.* New York, NY: Bt Bound.

McGovern, A. (1997). The *lady in the box.* New York, NY: Turtle Books.

Wolf, B. (1995). *Homeless.* New York, NY: Orchard Books.

Adolescent

Erlbaum, J. (2006). *Girlbomb: A halfway homeless memoir.* New York, NY: Villard Books.

Brenner, S. (2000). *Ivy: Tale of a homeless girl in San Francisco.* San Francisco, CA: Creative Art Book Company.

ERIC Digests

Abdal-Haqq, I. (1993). *Integrated services: New roles for schools, new challenges for teacher education.* ED355197 Feb 93. ERIC Digest. Washington, DC: ERIC Clearinghouse on Teacher Education.
http://eric.ed.gov/ERICDocs/data/ericdocs2/content_storage_01/0000000b/80/2a/1e/13.pdf

ERIC Development Team (1991). *Highly mobile students: Educational problems and possible solutions.* ERIC/CUE Digest #73 Jun 91. New York, NY: ERIC Clearinghouse on Urban Education.
http://eric.ed.gov/ERICDocs/data/ericdocs2/content_storage_01/0000000b/80/2a/15/98.pdf

Goins, B. & Cesarone, B. (1993). *Homeless children: Meeting the educational challenges.* ED356099 93. ERIC Digest. Urbana, IL: ERIC Clearinghouse on Elementary and Early Childhood Education.
http://eric.ed.gov/ERICDocs/data/ericdocs2/content_storage_01/0000000b/80/2a/1e/67.pdf

Heflin, L.J. (1991). *Developing effective programs for special education students who are homeless.* ED340148 Nov 91. ERIC Digest #E504. Reston, VA: ERIC Clearinghouse on Handicapped and Gifted Children.
http://eric.ed.gov/ERICDocs/data/ericdocs2/content_storage_01/0000000b/80/2a/15/dc.pdf

Imel, S. (1993). *Education for homeless adults.* ED358376 93. ERIC Digest. Columbus, OH: ERIC Clearinghouse on Adult, Career, and Vocational Education.
http://www.ed.gov/databases/ERIC_Digests/ed358376.html

Klauke, A. (1989). *Coping with changing demographics.* ED315865 89. ERIC Digest Series Number EA45. Eugene, OR: ERIC Clearinghouse on Educational Management. http://www.ed.gov/databases/ERIC_Digests/ed315865.html

Schwartz, W. (1995). *School programs and practices for homeless students.* ED383783 Apr 95. ERIC/CUR Digest, No. 105. New York: ERIC Clearinghouse on Urban Education.
http://eric.ed.gov/ERICDocs/data/ericdocs2/content_storage_01/0000000b/80/2a/23/50.pdf

Schwartz, W. (1995). *A guide to promoting children's education in homeless families, for parents/about parents.* ED396015. New York, NY: ERIC Clearinghouse on Urban Education.
http://eric.ed.gov/ERICDocs/data/ericdocs2/content_storage_01/0000000b/80/26/9e/7a.pdf

Vissing, Y.M. (1999). *Homeless children: Addressing the challenge in rural schools.* ED425046 Jan 99. ERIC Digest. Charleston, WV: ERIC Clearninghouse on Rural Education and Small Schools.
http://eric.ed.gov/ERICDocs/data/ericdocs2/content_storage_01/0000000b/80/2a/2c/78.pdf

Walls, C.A. (2003). *Providing highly mobile students with an effective education.* ED482918 Nov 03. New York, NY:ERIC Clearinghouse on Urban Education.
http://eric.ed.gov/ERICDocs/data/ericdocs2/content_storage_01/0000000b/80/2a/3b/7a.pdf

Wells, A.S. (1989). *Educating homeless children.* ED308276. ERIC/CUE Digest No. 52 1989. New York, NY: ERIC Clearinghouse on Urban Education.
http://eric.ed.gov/ERICDocs/data/ericdocs2/content_storage_01/0000000b/80/2a/0f/12.pdf

Videos

Almost Home (1996, 25 minutes). Directed by C. Wade, Boston, MA: Fanlight Productions. Available from Fanlight Productions, 4196 Washington Street, Suite 2, Boston, MA 02131. (617)469-4999. email: orders@fanlight.com. Website: www.fanlight.com.

The Art and Poetry of the Homeless (1995, 30 minutes). Produced by R. Chambers. Derry, NH: Chip Taylor Communications. Available from: Chip Taylor Communications, 2 East View Drive, Derry, NH 03038. (800)876-CHIP.
Website: www.chiptaylor.com.

Consumers Working as Providers: Improving Quality and Reducing Costs (1997, 61 minutes). Produced by D. B. Fisher, & A. Long. Lawrence, MA: The National Empowerment Center, Inc. Available from: National Empowerment Center, Inc., 599 Canal Street, Lawrence, MA 08140. (800)POWER-2-U. Website: www.power2u.com

Dark Days (2001, 84 minutes). Directed by M. Singer. New York, NY: Palm Pictures. Available   from: www.amazon.com/exec/obidos/ASIN/B0000A1HRS/wwwpalmpictur-2/103-6935927-2405418.

Don't Make Me Choose (1993, 17 minutes). Produced by and available from Night Vision Productions. South Windsor, CT: Night Vision. Available from: Night Vision Productions, Inc., P.O. Box 61, West Haven, CT 06516, (203)937-6088. Website: www.lorriewesoly.com.

Down and Out in America (1987). Produced by Joseph Feury Productions, Oak Forest, IL: MPI Home Video. Video 21262-H, Shapiro Film & Video Library, B700 School of Social Work Building, 1080 S. University, The University of Michigan, Ann Arbor MI 48109-1106. (734)764-5169. email: social.work.library@umich.edu. Website: http://www.lib.umich.edu.socwork/

Even You (undated, 30 minutes). Produced by Cleveland Municipal School District, Project ACT, 2373 East 30th Street, Cleveland, OH 44115. (216)592-7405. FAX: (216)592-7410. email: info@projectact.com.

Faces Of Homelessness (1991, 32 minutes). Produced by the Massachusetts Department of Education, Office for the Education of Homeless Children and Youth, 350 Main Street, Malden, Massachusetts 02148. (617)388-3300, Ext. 382.

The Faces of Homelessness (2000, 14 minutes). Produced by National Coalition for the Homeless. Washington, DC: The National Coalition for the Homeless. Available from the National Coalition for the Homeless, 1012 14th Street, NW, #600, Washington, DC 20005. (202)737-6444. Website: www.natinalhomeless.org.

Facing the Challenge: Building Peer Programs for Street Youth (1996, 24 minutes). Produced by Children's Hospital Los Angeles. Available from: Division of Adolescent Medicine, Children's Hospital Los Angeles, 4650 Sunset Boulevard #2, Los Angeles, CA 90027. (213)669-4506. Website: www.childrenshospitalla.org.

Fall of the I Hotel (1993). Produced by C. Choy. San Francisco, CA: Distributed by NAATA. Video 37601-H, Shapiro Film & Video Library, B700 School of Social Work Building, 1080 S. University, The University of Michigan, Ann Arbor MI 48109-1106. (734)764-5169. email: social.work.library@umich.edu. Website: http://www.lib.umich.edu.socwork/

First Monday: Bringing Justice Home (1999, 30 minutes). Directed by G. Pearcy. Washington, DC: Alliance for Justice. Available from: Alliance for Justice, 11 Dupont Circle, NW, 2nd Floor, Washington, DC 20036. (202)822-6070. email: fmonday@afj.org

From the Other Side (1992, 30 minutes). Directed by W.W. Moxam, Winnipeg, Canada: Winnipeg Film Group. Available from: The Winnipeg Film Group, 304-100 Arthur Street, Winnipeg, Manitoba, Canada R3B 1H3. (204)925-3455. Website: www.winnipegfilmgroup.mb.ca/index.cfm?FS=0&CF=1.

The Healing Place (1985, 40 minutes). Produced by Jefferson County Medical Society Outreach Program. Louisville, KY: Jefferson County Medical Society Outreach Program. Available from: The Healing Place, 1020 West Market Street, Louisville, KY 40202. (502)584-6606. email: thp@thehealingplace.org. Website: www.thehealingplace.org.

Healthcare for the Homeless (1994, 33 minutes). Directed by B. Achtenberg. Boston, MA: Fanlight Productions. Available from: Fanlight Productions, 4196 Washington

Street, Suite 2, Boston, MA 02131. (617)469-4999. email: orders@fanlight.com.
Website: www.fanlight.com

Health Care for the Homeless: An Introduction (2001, 20 minutes). Produced by National
Health Care for the Homeless Council. Nashville, TN: National Health Care for the
Homeless Council., Available from: National Health Care for the Homeless Coun-
cil, P.O. Box 60427, Nashville, TN 37206. (615)226-2292.
Website: www.nhchc.org/publications.

Health Care for the Homeless: Outreach (2001, 21 minutes).). Produced by National
Health Care for the Homeless Council. Nashville, TN: National Health Care for the
Homeless Council., Available from: National Health Care for the Homeless Coun-
cil, P.O. Box 60427, Nashville, TN 37206. (615)226-2292.
Website: www.nhchc.org/publications.

Healthcare for the Homeless: You Must Never Give Up (1991, 33 minutes). Directed by
B. Achtenberg. Boston, MA: Fanlight Productions. Available from: Fanlight Productions, 4196 Washington Street, Suite 2, Boston, MA 02131. (617)469-4999.
email: orders@fanlight.com. Website: www.fanlight.com

A Homecoming (1998, 57 minutes). Produced by R. Brewin, K. Hartman, K. Johnson, K.,
& A. Lindrup, Chicago, IL: Unitarian Universalist Social Concerns. Available From:
Unitarian Universalist Social Concerns, 1448 East 52nd Street, Box 144, Chicago,
IL 60615. (773)643-8122. email: uuscaj1@enteract.com.
Website: http://members.tripod.com/uusocialconcerns.

A Home In Between: Designing Transitional Housing For Women And Children (1992,
13 minutes). Produced and directed by Maguire/Reeder, Ltd. Available from the National Coalition for the Homeless, 1012 14th Street, NW, #600, Washington, DC
20005. (202)737-6444. Website: www.natinalhomeless.org.

The Homeless: I Too Have A Dream (undated, 10 minutes). Produced by the Hawaii Department of Education. Honolulu, HW: Hawaii Department of Education. Available
from: Hawaii Department of Education, 2530 10th Avenue, Room A-15, Honolulu,
Hawaii 96816. (808)735-9024.

Home Less Home (1991, 70 minutes). Available from Bill Brand Productions, 108 Frank-
lin Street, 34W, New York, NY 10013. (212)966-6253. email:
bbrand@pipeline.com Website: www.bboptics.com/homelesshome.html.

The Homeless Homer Movie (1997, 85 minutes). Directed by P. Hennessey. Minneapolis,
MN: Media Visions, Inc. Available from: Media Visions, 108 8th Avenue South,
South Saint Paul, MN 55075. email: mvisions@bitstream.net.
Website: http://marley.bitstream.net/~mvisions/.

Homeless In America (undated, 12 minutes). Produced by National Mental Health Association. Alexandria, VA: National mental Health Association. Available from the
National Mental Health Association, 2001 North Beauregard Street, 12 Floor, Alexandria, VA 22311. (703)684-7722. Website: www.nmha.org.

Homeless in America: Bring Your Best, Parts 1 and 2 (1995, 45 minutes). Produced by
Sharp Productions, Inc. Derry, NH: Sharp Productions, Inc. Available from: Chip
Taylor Communications, 2 East View Drive, Derry, NH 03038-4812. (800)876-
CHIP.
Website: www.shiptaylor.com.

Homeless to Harvard: The Liz Murray Story (2003, 120 minutes). Directed by P. Levin,
New York, NY: Lifetime Entertainment Services. Available from: National Resource Center on Homelessness and Mental Illness, 7500 Old Georgetown Road
#900, Bethesda, MD 20814. (800)444-7415. email: nrtc@cdmgroup.com .

Website: www.nrcmhi.samhsa.gov.

Home Street Home (1988). NBC News, Chicago, IL: Films, Inc. Video 13019-H Shapiro Film & Video Library, B700 School of Social Work Building, 1080 S. University, The University of Michigan, Ann Arbor MI 48109-1106. (734)764-5169. email: social.work.library@umich.edu. Website: http://www.lib.umich.edu.socwork/

Houseless Not Hopeless (1990, 29 minutes). Produced by NEWIST/CESA 7. Green Bay, WI: NEWIST/CESA 7. Available from: University of Wisconsin, IS 1040, Greenbay, WI 54311. (920)465-2599. email: newest@uwgb.edu.

I'm Every Woman (1994, 70 minutes). Produced by Homeless Health Care Los Angeles. Los Angeles, CA: Homeless Health Care Los Angeles. Available from: Homeless Health Care Los Angeles, Available from: National Resource Center on Homelessness and Mental Illness, 7500 Old Georgetown Road #900, Bethesda, MD 20814. (800)444-7415. email: nrtc@cdmgroup.com . Website: www.nrcmhi.samhsa.gov.

In Our Backyard (1996, 18 minutes). Directed by L. Platt. New York, NY: Corporation for Supportive Housing. Available from: Corporation for Supportive Housing, 50 Broadway, 17th Floor, New York, NY 10004. (212)986-2966. Website: www.csh.org.

I Want To Go Home -- Homeless in New Hampshire (1991, 20 minutes). Produced by C. Enos, & Y. Vissing. Portsmouth, NH: Video Verite. Available from Video Verite, Attn: Peter Braddock, PO Box 1579, Portsmouth, NH 03802. (603)436-3360.

It Was A Wonderful Life -- Hidden Homeless Women (1993, 52 minutes). Produced by Filmakers Library. New York, NY: Filmakers Library. Available from Filmmakers Library, Inc., 124 E. 40th St., New York, NY 10016. (212)808-4980. FAX: (212)808-4983. Website: www.filmakers.com

Lost In The Shuffle: Homeless Children In Our Schools (undated, 15 minutes). Produced by Illinois State Board of Education. Springfield, IL: Illinois State Board of Education, Available from: Illinois State Board of Education, 100 N. 1st Street, Springfield, IL 62777. (312)814-3616.

Love Can Build a Bridge (1995, 5 minutes). Produced by Comic Relief, Inc. Los Angeles, CA: Comic Relief Inc. Available from: Comic Relief Inc, 6404 Wilshire Blvd., #960, Los Angeles, CA 90048.

Mansions Above (1994). Produced by McKinney Education Project. Sioux Falls, SD: McKinney Education Project. Available from: Edison Middle School, 2101 S. West Ave., Sioux Falls, SD 57105.

Miracle on 43rd Street (1997, 60 minutes) Produced by 60 Minutes. New York, NY: CBS Television Network. Available from: Burrelle's Transcripts, P.O. Box 7, Livingston, NJ 07039. (800)777-8389. email: transcripts@burrelles.com.

Miracle on South Michigan Street (1996). South Bend, IN: Golden Dome Productions. Video 27466-H, Shapiro Film & Video Library, B700 School of Social Work Building, 1080 S. University, The University of Michigan, Ann Arbor MI 48109-1106. (734)764-5169. email: social.work.library@umich.edu. Website: http://www.lib.umich.edu.socwork/

Neighbors in Need (1991, 42 minutes). Directed by B. Wilson. Los Angeles, CA: California Homeless and Housing Coalition. Available from: National Resource Center on Homelessness and Mental Illness, 7500 Old Georgetown Road #900, Bethesda, MD 20814. (800)444-7415. email: nrtc@cdmgroup.com Website: www.nrcmhi.samhsa.gov.

No Place Like Home (1993). Produced by K. Hunt, Berkeley, CA: University of California Extension Center for Media and Independent Learning. Video 26994-H, Shapiro Film & Video Library, B700 School of Social Work Building, 1080 S. University,

The University of Michigan, Ann Arbor MI 48109-1106. (734)764-5169. email: social.work.library@umich.edu.
Website: http://www.lib.umich.edu.socwork/

Paper House (1990, 5 minutes). Produced by Fanlight Productions Media Library. Boston, MA: Fanlight Productions. Available from: Fanlight Productions, 4196 Washington Street, Suite 2, Boston, MA 02131. (617)469-4999. email: orders@fanlight.com Website: www.fanlight.com.

Peter, Donald, Willie, Pat (1988, 30 minutes). Produced by M. Majoros & J. Kaufman. Boston, MA: Fanlight Productions. Available from: Fanlight Productions 4196 Washington Street, Suite 2, Boston, MA 02131. (617)469-4999. email: orders@fanlight.com. Website: www.fanlight.com.

Pieces of the Puzzle (1997, 20 minutes). Produced by the STAR Center at the Charles A. Dana Center, The University of Texas, 2901 North IH-35, Suite 3.200, Austin, TX 78722-2348. (512)475-9702.

Project H.O.M.E. (1998, 22 minutes). Produced by Project H.O.M.E. Philadelphia, PA: Shirley Road Productions. Available from: Project H.O.M.E., 1515 Fairmount Avenue, Philadelphia, PA 19130. (215)232-7272. Website: www.projecthome.net.

Project Hope (1998, 12 minutes). Produced by Project Hope. Phoenix, AZ: Project Hope. Available from: Project Hope, 255 Carter Hall Lane, Millwood, VA 22646. (540)837-2100. Website: www.projecthope.org

Promises to Keep (1988). Washington, DC: Durrin Productions, Inc. Video 13572-H, Shapiro Film & Video Library, B700 School of Social Work Building, 1080 S. University, The University of Michigan, Ann Arbor MI 48109-1106. (734)764-5169. email: social.work.library@umich.edu. Website: http://www.lib.umich.edu.socwork/

Reach For The Child (1991, 29 minutes). Produced by the Media Resources Center-Iowa State University. Des Moines, IA: Media Resources Center- Iowa State University. Available from: Iowa Department of Education, Grimes State Office Building, Des Moines, Iowa 50319-0146. (515)281-3966.

Reach Out, Teach One: The Peer Educators Project in Action (2000, 25 minutes). Produced by Mental Illness Education Project, Inc. Brookline Village, MA: The Mental Illness Education Project, Inc. Available from: The Mental Illness Education Project, Inc., P.O. Box 470813, Brookline Village, MA 02447. (617)562-1111. Website: www.miepvideos.org.

Rewind: It Could Have Been Me (1994, 13 minutes). Directed by L. Loch. Hudson, NY: Morning Glory Films. Available from: National Coalition for the Homeless, 1012 14th Street, NW, #600, Washington, DC 20005. (202)737-6444. Website: www.nationalhomeless.org.

The Road Home (1994, 15 minutes). Directed by B. Jones. Charlotte, NC: Mecklenburg County Department of Mental Health. Available from: National Resource Center on Homelessness and Mental Illness, 7500 Old Georgetown Road #900, Bethesda, MD 20814.   (800)444-7415.   email: nrtc@cdmgroup.com   .   Website: www.nrcmhi.samhsa.gov.

San Fernando Valley Mobile Homeless Center (undated, 4 minutes). Produced by Los Angeles Family Housing Corporation. North Hollywood, CA: Los Angeles Family Housing Corporation. Available from: Los Angeles Family Housing Corporation, 7843 Lankershim Boulevard, North Hollywood, CA 91605. (818)982-4091.

A Safe Place: Creating Safe Havens Training Video (undated, 45 minutes). Produced by United States Department of Housing and Urban Development. Washington, DC: U.S. Department of Housing and Urban Development. Available from: HUD, 451 7th Street, SW, Washington, DC 20410. (202)708-1112. Website: www.hud.org.

The Salt Mines (1990). Produced by S. Aikin and C. Aparicio, San Francisco, CA: Frameline. Video 34117-H, Shapiro Film & Video Library, B700 School of Social Work Building, 1080 S. University, The University of Michigan, Ann Arbor MI 48109-1106. (734)764-5169. email: social.work.library@umich.edu.
Website: http://www.lib.umich.edu.socwork/

School for the Homeless (2001, 13 minutes) Produced by 60 Minutes. New York, NY: CBS Television Network. Available from: Burelle's Transcripts, P.O. Box 7, Livingston, NJ 07039. (800)848-3256.

Second Chances: A Model for Change (1994, 21 minutes). Produced by West Los Angeles Veterans Medical Center. Los Angeles, CA: Visionworks Entertainment, LLC. Available from: National Resource Center on Homelessness and Mental Illness, 7500 Old Georgetown Road #900, Bethesda, MD 20814. (800)444-7415. FAX: (301)656-4012. email: nrct@cdmgroup.com Website: www.nrcmhi.samhsa.gov

Serving as a Representative Payee (1992, 18 minutes). Produced by Social Security Administration. Baltimore, MD: Social Security Administration. Available from: Social Security Administration, Office of Public Inquiries, Windsor Park Building, 6401 Security Boulevard, Baltimore, MD 21235. (800)772-1213. Website: www.ssa.gov.

Shelter Boy (Circa 1989, 15 minutes). Produced by Fox Television. New York, NY: Fox Television. Available from "The Reporters," Fox Television, 205 East 67th Street, New York, NY 10021.

Shelter Stories (1990, 14 minutes). Directed by M. Perlson. Boston, MA: Fanlight Productions. Available from: Fanlight Productions, 4196 Washington Street, Suite 2, Boston, MA 02131. (617)469-4999.
email: orders@fanlight.com. Website: www.fanlight.com.

Shirley Mann's Story (1995, 11 minutes). Produced by Community Action Board of Santa Cruz, Inc. Available from: Community Action Board of Santa Cruz, Inc., 501 Soquel Avenue, Suite E, Santa Cruz, CA 95062. (831)457-1741. Website: www.cabinc.org

Shooting Back (1990, 30 minutes). Produced by Fanlight Productions Media Library. Boston, MA: Fanlight Productions Media Library. Available from: Fanlight Productions, 4196 Washington Street, Suite 2, Boston, MA 02131. (617)469-4999.
email: orders@fanlight.com Website: www.fanlight.com

Simple Giving (undated, 12 minutes). Albuquerque, NM: Albuquerque Health Care for the Homeless. Video #10022 Available from National Resource Center on Homelessness and Mental Illness, 7500 Old Georgetown Road #900, Bethesda, MD 20814. (800)444-7415. FAX: (301)656-4012.
email: nrtc@cdmgroup.com. Website: http://www.nremhi.samhsa.gov

Six Homeless Programs (1999, 134 minutes). Produced by Health Care for the Homeless Information Resource Center. Delmar, NY: HCH Information Resource Center. Available from: Health Care for the Homeless Information Resource Center, 345 Delaware Avenue, Delmar, NY 12054. (888)439-3300. Website: www.,bphc.hrsa.gov/hchirc.

St. Anthony's: Making the Connections (1990, 23 minutes). Produced by St. Anthony Foundation. Los Angeles, CA: Franciscan Communications. Available from: St. Anthony Foundation, 121 Golden Gate Avenue, San Francisco, CA 94102. (415)241-2600. Website: www.stanthonysf.org/homeflash.html.

Street Life: The Invisible Family (1988, 58 minutes). Produced by V. Verdoia & S. Chaffin. Boston, MA: Fanlight Productions. Available from: Fanlight Productions, 4196

Washington Street, Suite 2, Boston, MA 02131. (617)469-4909.
email: orders@fanlight.com. Website: www.fanlight.com.

Street Talk and Tuxes (1998, 55 minutes). Produced by S. Shadburne. Hohokus, NJ: Susan Shadburne Productions. Available from: Susan Shadburne Productions, LLC, 1221 Northwest Summit Avenue, Portland, OR 97210. (503)222-6676.

Supportive Housing: Mainstream/Main Street (undated, 15 minutes). Produced by Collaborative Support Program of New Jersey. Available from: Collaborative Support Program of New Jersey, 30 Broad Street, Freehold, NJ 07728. (732)780-1175.

Surviving Friendly Fire (2000). Directed by T. Nelson. San Francisco, CA: Frameline Distribution. Available from: Frameline Distribution, 145 Ninth Street, Suite 300, San Francisco CA 94103. (415)703-8655. Website: www.frameline.org/distribution.

Survivors Of The Streets: Success Stories Of Four Who Were Homeless (1992, 28 minutes). Produced by C. Slater. Stanford, CT: Full Circle Productions, Inc. Available from Full Circle Productions, 87 Glenbrook Road, Stanford, CT 06902. (203)961-1402.
Website: www.fullcp.com

Taking it From the Streets (1993, 45 minutes). Produced by Paragon. Orange County, CA: Paragon. Available from: National Resource Center on Homelessness and Mental Illness, 7500 Old Georgetown Road #900, Bethesda, MD 20814. (800)444-7415.
email: nrtc@cdmgroup.com. Website: www.nrcmhi.samhsa.gov.

Taylor's Campaign (1998, 72 minutes). Directed by R Cohen. Venice, CA: Richard Cohen Films. Available from: Richard Cohen Films, P.O. Box 1012, Venice, CA 90294. (310)395-3549. Website: www.richardcohenfilms.com/taylor's.htm

Under Power: Vision and Change (undated, 22 minutes). Produced by Chicago Health Outreach. Chicago, IL: Chicago Health Outreach. Available from: Chicago Health Outreach, 4750 N. Sheridan Road, Suite 500, Chicago, IL 60640. (773)275-2586. Website: www.heartland-alliance.org.

Under The Bridge (undated, 9 minutes). Hoffman Estates, IL: American City Bureau. Available from: American City Bureau, Inc., 33 West Higgins road, Suite 520, South Barrington, IL 60010. (224)293-3000. Website: www.acb-inc.com.

Video Resume (1995, 8 minutes). Produced by Community Action Board of Santa Cruz, Inc. Available from: Community Action Board of Santa Cruz, Inc., 501 Soquel Avenue, Suite E, Santa Cruz, CA 95062. (831)457-1741. Website: www.cabinc.org

We Don't Leave our Wounded Behind: A Program for Homeless Veterans (undated, 17 minutes). Produced by Disabled American Veterans, Washington, DC: Disabled American Veterans. Available from: National Resource Center on Homelessness and Mental Illness, 7500 Old Georgetown Road #900, Bethesda, MD 20814. (800)444-7415.
email: nrtc@cdmgroup.com . Website: www.nrcmhi.samhsa.gov.

West 47th Street (2003, 60 minutes). Directed by B. Lichtenstein. New York, NY: Lichtenstein Creative Media, 25 West 36th Street, 11th Floor, New York, NY 10018. (800)PLAY-PBS. Website: www.LCMedia.com.

What Does a Person Deserve? (1999, 2 minutes). Directed by K. Kimmelman. New York, NY: Imagery Film, Ltd. Available from: Imagery Film, Ltd., 91 Bedford Street, Suite 1-R, New York, NY 10014. (212)243-5579. email: ifl@mindspring.com.
Website: http://ifl.home.mindspring.com.

What's Wrong with This Picture? (1995, 28 minutes). Produced by C. B. Calhoun. Boston, MA: Fanlight Productions, Available from: Fanlight Productions, 4196 Wash-

ington Street, Suite 2, Boston, MA 02131. (617)469-4999. email: orders@fanlight.com.
Website: www.fanlight.com.

Why I Am Homeless (1995, 9 minutes). Produced by Community Action Board of Santa Cruz, Inc. Available from: Community Action Board of Santa Cruz, Inc., 501 Soquel Avenue, Suite E, Santa Cruz, CA 95062. (831)457-1741. Website: www.cabinc.org

Women of Hope (1989, 22 minutes). Produced by T. Brown and C. Bottinelli. Philadelphia, PA: WCAU TV. Available from: Films for the Humanities and Sciences, P.O. Box 2053, Princeton, NJ 08543. (800)257-5126. Website: www.films.com.

Women Speak Out (1999, 40 minutes). Directed by M. Harris. Washington, DC: Community Connections. Available from: Community Connections, 801 Pennsylvania Avenue SE, Suite 201, Washington, DC 20003. Contact: Rebecca Wolfson, (202)608-4791. Website: www.communityconnectionsdc.org/publications.htm.

Internet Resources

Education

The Charles A. Dana Center: http://www-tenet.cc.utexas.edu/pub/dana/programs.html

Government

US Census Bureau: http://www.census.gov/
US Department of Education: http://www.ed.gov/
US Department of Housing and Urban Development: http://www.hud.gov/
The US Department of Housing and Urban Development's Office of Policy Development and Research (PD&R): http://www.huduser.org/index.html

Housing

***Information about joining the homeless email discussion list and accessing the list archives can be found at:* gopher://csf.colorado.edu/00/csf-lists/homeless/information.

Alabama Arise: http://www.mindspring.com/~stanjj/arise.html
Arkansas Low Income Housing Coalition: http://www.aristotle.net/alihc/
Center for Homeless Education and Information at William Penn College: http://www.wmpenn.edu/PennWeb/LTP/LTP2.html
Chicago Coalition for the Homeless: http://enteract.com/~cch/
Emergency Food and Shelter National Board Program: http://www.efsp.unitedway.org/
Florida Housing Coalition: http://www.nettally.com/fhc/
Georgia Coalition to End Homelessness/Atlanta Task Force on the Homeless: http://www.leveller.org/
Habitat for Humanity International: http://www.habitat.org/
Handsnet on the Web: http://www.handsnet.org/handsnet/index.html

HOMELESS HOME PAGE at Communications for a Sustainable Future:
    http://csf.colorado.edu/homeless/index.html
Homes for the Homeless: http://www.opendoor.com/hfh/
The Housing Assistance Council: http://www.ruralhome.org/
The International Union of Gospel Missions: http://www.iugm.org/
Michigan Coalition Against Homelessness:
    http://comnet.org/local/orgs/MCAH/index.html
Minnesota Housing Partnership: http://www.mtn.org/mhpage/
The National Coalition for Homeless Veterans: http://www.nchv.org/
The National Coalition for the Homeless: http://www2.ari.net/home/nch/
The National Law Center on Homelessness and Poverty: http://www.tomco.net/~nlchp/
The National Low Income Housing Coalition: http://www.handsnet.org/nlihc/
The Stewart B. McKinney Homeless Assistance Act:
    http://www.law.cornell.edu/uscode/42/ch119.html
STREETKID-L Resource "Street Children" Online Organization Links
    **Instructions on joining the STREETKID-L email discussion list, along with other
    relevant links, can be found at: http://www.jbu.edu/business/sk.html
Texas Homeless Network: http://www.thn.org/
Texas Low Income Housing Information Service: http://uts.cc.utexas.edu/~txlihis/
Wyoming Coalition for the Homeless: http://www.wch.vcn.com/

Poverty

National Center for Children in Poverty: http://cpmcnet.columbia.edu/dept/nccp/
The Welfare Information Network: http://www.welfareinfo.org/

Public Policy

Center on Budget and Policy Priorities: http://www.cbpp.org/
Children's Defense Fund: http://www.childrensdefense.org
The Urban Institute: http://www.urban.org/
The US Conference of Mayors: http://www.usmayors.org/USCM/home.html

Organizations

Center on Budget and Policy Priorities
    820 First Street, NE Suite 510
    Washington, DC 20002
The Charles A. Dana Center
    The University of Texas at Austin
    2901 North IH-35, Suite 3.200
    Austin, TX 78722-2348
    Phone: 512/471-6190
    Fax: 512/471-6193
Children's Defense Fund
    25 E Street NW

Washington, DC 20001
Phone: 202/628-8787
Email: cdfinfo@childrensdefense.org
Feed The Children
333 Worth Meridian, POB 36
Oklahoma City, OK 73107
Phone: 405/942-0228
Fax: 405/945-4142
National Coalition for the Homeless
1612 K Street, NW, #1004
Washington, DC 20006
Phone: 202/775-1322
Fax: 202/775-1316
Email: nch@ari.net
National Law Center on Homelessness & Poverty
918 F St. NW, #412
Washington, DC 20004
Phone: 202/638-2535
Fax: 202/628-2737
Email: HN0749@handsnet.org
Reading Is Fundamental
600 Maryland Avenue, SW
Washington, DC 20024
Phone: 202/287-3220
Fax: 202/287-3196
The United States Conference of Mayors
1620 Eye Street, NW
Washington, DC 20006
Phone: 202/293-7330
Fax: 202/293-2352
The Urban Institute
Public Affairs
2100 M Street NW
Washington, DC 20037
Phone: 202/857-8709
Email: paffairs@ui.urban.org

Bibliography

Allington, R.L. & Johnston, P.H. (2002). Integrated instruction in exemplary fourth-grade classrooms. In Allington and Johnston (Eds.), *Reading to learn: Lessons from exemplary fourth-grade classrooms.* New York, NY: Guilford. 169-187.

The Annie E. Casey Foundation (2000). *Kids count census data analysis.* Baltimore, MD: Population Reference Bureau. Retrieved 3/8/04 from http://www.aecf.org/cgi-bin/aeccensus.cgi.

Aristotle (unknown). Retrieved 12/6/2006 from http://www.freerepublic.com/forum/A39eca0906518.htm.

Bandura, A. (1996). *Self-Efficacy: The exercise of control.* New York, NY: Freeman.

Bassuk, E. (1996). The characteristics and needs of sheltered homeless and low-income housed mothers. *Journal of the American medical association,* 276(8). 640-646.

Bauman, R. (1982). Ethnography of children's folklore. In Gilmore & Glatthorn (Eds.), *Children in and out of school, ethnography and education.* Washington, D.C.: Center for Applied Linguistics. 172-186.

Bernstein, D.K. (1986). The development of humor: Implications for assessment and intervention. *Topics in language disorders* (1). 47-58.

Blair, G.R. (2005). *Helping your kids set goals.* Retrieved 6/5/04 from www.FamilyFirst.net/parenting/goalsguy.asp

Bronfenbrenner, U. (1970). *Two worlds of childhood: U.S. and U.S.S.R.* New York, NY: Russell Sage Foundation. i.

Bruner, J. (1994). The 'remembered' self. In Neisser and Fivush, (Eds.), *The remembering self: Construction and accuracy in the self-narrative.* Cambridge, MA: Cambridge University Press. 41-54.

Bykofsky, S.D. (December 1, 1986). *Newsweek Magazine.* 12-13.

Center for Public Policy Priorities (2005). The state of Texas children 2005. In *Texas kids count annual data book.* Austin, TX: Texas University.

Children's Defense Fund (2003a). *Children in Texas.* Washington, D.C. Retrieved

6/05/06 from http://www.childrensdefense.org/data/childreninthestates/tx.

Children's Defense Fund (2003b). *2003 Facts on child poverty in America.* Washington, D.C. Retrieved 4/22/05 from http://www.childrensdefense.org/familyincome/childpoverty/basicfacts.aspx.

Children's Defense Fund (2004a). *Educational resource disparities for minority and low-income children..* Washington, D.C. Retrieved 4/22/05 from http://www.childrensdefense.org.

Children's Defense Fund (2004b). *The road to dropping out, Minority students & academic factors correlated with failure to complete high school.* Washington, D.C. Retrieved 4/22/05 from http://www.childrensdefense.org.

Chithprabha, K. (2005). Letter to a teacher by schoolboys of Barbiana: A forgotten treatise on school education. *Thinking classroom, 6(2).* Newark, DE: International Reading Association. 29-35.

Clay, M.M. (1989). Involving teachers in classroom research. In Pinnell and Matlin (Eds.), *Teachers and research, language learning in the classroom.* Newark, DE: International Reading Association. 29-46.

Clay, M.M. (1991). *Becoming literate: The construction of inner control.* Portsmouth, NH: Heinemann.

Church, E.B. (2003). Development ages & stages 5 to 6: Say it loud-say it clear. *Scholastic early childhood today,* 17(5). 28-29.

Cookson, P.W. (2005). Creating a civic culture. Teaching K-8. February 2005. Norwalk, CT: Early Years, Inc. 10

Cooley, M. (1992). *City aphorisms,* 10th selection. In Andrews, Biggs & Seidel (Eds). The Columbia World of Quotations. New York, NY: Columbia University Press, 2006. eNotes.com. 2006. Retrieved 12/12/2006 from http://history.enotes.com/famous-quotes/

Crystal, D. (1998). *Language play.* London, England: Penguin Books.

Davies, B. & Harre, R. (1999). Positioning and personhood. In Harre & Langenhove (Eds.), *Positioning theory: Moral contexts of intentional action.* Oxford, England: Blackwell. 32-52.

Delpit, L. (1988). The silenced dialogue: Power and pedagogy in educating other people's children. *Harvard educational review,* 58(3). 280-298.

Dyson, A.H. (1999). Coach Bombay's kids learn to write: Children's appropriation of media material for school literacy. *Research in the teaching of English,* 33(4). 396-397.

Donaldson, M. (1978). *Children's minds.* New York, NY: W. W. Norton.

Edelman, M.W. (1989). As quoted in *I dream a world,* by Brian Lanker.

Elton, L. (1996). Strategies to enhance student motivation: a conceptual analysis. *Studies in higher education,* 21(1). 57-67.

Finn, J.D. & Cox, D. (1992). Participation and withdrawal among fourth-grade pupils. *American educational research journal,* 29(1). 141-162.

Fleischer, K.H., & Belgredan, J.H. (1990). An overview of judgment-based assessment. *Topics in early childhood special education,* 10(3). 13-23.

Fowles, B. & Glanz, M.E. (1976). Competence and talent in verbal riddle comprehension. *Journal of child language,* 4. 433-452.

Freud, S. (1991). *Jokes and their relation to the unconscious.* London, England: Penguin Library. Original publication, 1905.

Fulghum, R. (1988). *It was on fire when I lay down on it.* New York, NY: Ivy Books. Copyright © 1988, 1989 by Robert Fulghum. Used by permission of Villard Books, a division of Random House, Inc.

Garson, G.D. (2006). *Ethnographic research*. North Carolina State University. Retrieved 6/6/2006 from http://www2.chass.ncsu.edu/garson/PA765/ethno.htm.

Geller, L.G. (1985). *Wordplay and language learning for children*. Urbana, IL: National Council of Teachers of English.

Genishi, Celia (1985). Observing communicative performance in young children. In Jaggar and Smith-Burke (Eds.), *Observing the language learner*. Newark, DE: International Reading Association and Urbana, IL: National Council of Teachers of English. 131-142.

Gershoff, E. (2003a). Low income and hardship among America's kindergartners. *Living at the edge research brief no. 3*. New York, NY: National Center for Children in Poverty, Columbia University Mailman School of Public Health.

Gershoff, E. (2003b). Low income and the development of American's kindergartners. *Living at the edge research brief no. 4*. New York, NY: National Center for Children in Poverty, Columbia University Mailman School of Public Health.

Goodman, K. (1996). Language development: Issues, insights, and implementation. In Power and Hubbard (Eds.), *Language development, A reader for teachers*. Englewood Cliffs, NJ: Prentice-Hall, Inc. 81-86.

Goodman, K. & Goodman, Y. (1978). *Reading of American children whose language is a stable rural dialect of English or language other than English* (Final report, Project NIE-C-00-3-0087). Washington, DC: U.S. Department of Health, Education, and Welfare, National Institute of Education.

Grisham, J. (1999). *The street lawyer*. New York, NY: Island Books, Published by Dell Publishing a division of Random House, Inc.

Haberman, M. (1995). *Star teachers of children in poverty*. West Lafayette, IN: Kappa Delta Pi International Honor Society in Education.

Haley, G. (1985). In Andrews, Biggs, & Seidel (Eds.). *The Columbia world of quotations*. New York, NY: Columbia University Press. Retrieved 12/13/2006 from http://history.enotes.com/famous-quotes/children-who-are-not-spoken-to-by-live-and>.

Halliday, M.A.K. (1973). The functional basis of language. In Bernstein (Ed.), *Class, codes, and control, volume 2, Applied studies toward a sociology of language*. Boston, MA: Routledge & Kegan Paul. 343-366.

Halliday, M.A.K. (1975). *Learning how to mean: Explorations in the development of language*. London, England: Edward Arnold Ltd.

Halliday, M.A.K. (1980). Three aspects of children's language development: Learning language, learning through language, learning about language. In Goodman, Haussler, and Strickland (Eds), *Oral and written language development research: Impact on the schools*. Urbana, IL: National Council of Teachers of English. 7-19.

Halliday, M.A.K. (1982). Relevant models of language. In B. Wade (Ed.), *Language perspectives*. London, England: Heinemann Educational Books. 37-49.

Halliday, M.A.K. (1994). *An introduction to functional grammar*. (2nd Ed.). London: Edward Arnold.

Harre, R. & Gillet, G. (1994). *The discursive mind*. Thousand Oaks, CA: Sage.

Harste, J., Woodward, V., & Burke, C. (1984). *Language stories and literacy lessons*. Portsmouth, NH: Heinemann.

Hart, B., & Risley T.R. (1995). *Meaningful differences in the everyday experiences of young American children*. Baltimore, MD: Paul H. Brookes Publishing Co.

Hartle-Schutte, D. (1993). Literacy development in Navajo homes: Does it lead to success in school?. *Language Arts*, 70(8). 642-654.

Hart-Shegos, E. (1999). *Homelessness and its effects on children.* Minneapolis, MN: Family Housing Fund.

Hasan, R. (1981). What's going on: A dynamic view of context in language. In Copeland (Ed.), *The seventh LACUS forum 1980.* Columbia, SC: Hernbeam Press. 106-121.

Haycock, K. (1998). Good teaching matters: How well-qualified teachers can close the gap. *Thinking K-16,* 3(2). Washington, D.C.: The Education Trust. 1-14.

Heath, S.B. (1983). *The invisible culture: Communication in classroom and community on the warm springs Indian reservation.* New York: Longman.

Heffner, C. (2002). Section 2, Maslow's hierarchy of needs; Chapter 10, Humanistic theory. *Personality synopsis.* Retrieved 4/18/05 from http://allpsych.com/personalitysynopsis/maslow.html

Higgins, Stegall & Crist (2004). The neglected half of teaching. In Flores, Hufford & Starlin (Eds). *Educating for peace: Cherishing diversity. Journal of interdisciplinary education* 6(1). San Antonio, TX: North America Chapter of the World Council for Curriculum and Instruction. 59-83.

Hymes, D. (1972). Introduction. In Cazden, John & Hymes (Eds.), *Functions of language in the classroom.* New York, NY: Teachers College Press.

Hymes, D. (1974). *Foundations in sociolinguistics: An ethnographic approach.* Philadelphia, PA: University of Pennsylvania Press.

Institute for Children in Poverty (1999). *Access to success: Meeting the educational needs of homeless children and families.* New York, NY.

Institute for Children in Poverty (2000). *Who are the homeless?* poster. New York, NY.

Irish, K.; Schumacher, R.; and Lombardi, J. (2003). *Head start comprehensive services: A key support for early learning.* Washington, DC: Center for Law and Social Policy.

Jaggar, A. (1985). On observing the language learner: Introduction and overview. In Jaggar and Smith-Burke (Eds.), *Observing the language learner.* Newark, DE: International Reading Association and Urbana, IL: National Council of Teachers of English. 1-7.

Jaggar, A. & Smith-Burke, M.T. (Eds.) (1985). *Observing the language learner.* Newark DE: International Reading Association and Urbana, IL: National Council of Teachers of English.

James, B.; Lopez, P.; Murdock, B.; Rouse, J.; & Walker, N. (1997). *Pieces of the puzzle.* Austin, TX: STAR (Support for Texas Academic Renewal) Center.

Jesse, L.E. (2006). City takes step toward new way to aid homeless. *Express News,* November 30, 2006. Retrieved 12/11/2006 from http://www.mysanantonio.com/news/citycouncil/stories/MYSA12106.01A. HomelessPlan

Johnston, P.H. (2004). *Choice words, how our language affects children's learning.* Portland, ME: Stenhouse Publishers.

Johnston, P.H. & Backer. J. (2002). Inquiry and a good conversation: 'I learn a lot from them'. In Allington and Johnston (Eds.), *Reading to learn: Lessons from exemplary fourth-grade classrooms.* New York, NY: Guilford. 37-53.

Johnston, P.H. & Quinlan, M.E. (2002). A caring, responsible learning community. In Allington & Johnston (Eds.), *Reading to learn: Lessons from exemplary fourth-grade classrooms.* New York, NY: Guilford. 123-139.

Johnston, P.H & Winograd, P.N. (1985). Passive failure in reading. *Journal of reading behavior* 17(4). 279-301.

Keniston, K. (1977). *All our children.* Ch 2. New York, NY: The Carnegie Council on Children.

Kiefer, B.Z. & DeStefano, J.S. (1985). Cultures together in the classroom: "What you sayin?". In Jaggar & Smith-Burke (Eds.), *Observing the language learner*. Newark, DE: International Reading Association and Urbana, IL: National Council of Teachers of English. 159-172.

King, H. (1994). *Crib Notes*. New York, NY: Avon Books.

King, M.L. (1985). Language and language learning for child watchers. In Jaggar & Smith-Burke (Eds.), *Observing the language learner*. Newark, DE: International Reading Association and Urbana, IL: National Council of Teachers of English. 19-38.

Kozol, J. (1988) *Rachel and her children; Homeless families in America*. New York, NY: Crown Publishers, Inc.

Kozol, J. (1995). *Amazing grace: The lives of children and the conscience of a nation*. New York, NY: Crown Publishers, Inc.

Kraljic, M.A. (Ed) (1992). *The homeless problem*. The reference shelf, 64(2). New York, NY: The H.W. Wilson Company.

Lefcourt, H.M. & Thomas, S. (1998). Humor and stress revisited. In Ruch, W. (Ed.), *The sense of humor: Explorations of a personality characteristic*. New York, NY: Mouton de Gruyter. 179-202.

Levitas, M. (1992). Homeless in America. In Kraljic, M. (Ed.) *The homeless problem*. The reference shelf, 64(2). New York, NY: The H.W. Wilson Company. 11-24.

Lindfors, J.W. (1985). Understanding the development of language structure. In Jaggar & Smith-Burke (Eds.), *Observing the language learner*. Newark, DE: International Reading Association and Urbana, IL: National Council of Teachers of English. 41-56.

Martson, S. (2005) *Thebalancing act*. Issue 7, July 2005. Retrieved 1/30/2007 from http://www.stephaniemarston.com/newsletters/july05.html.

Maslow, A.H. (1998). *Toward a psychology of being* (3rd Ed.). New York, NY: John Wiley & Sons.

Mayer, D.P.; Mullens, J.E.; & Moore, M.T. (2000). *Monitoring school quality: An indicators report* (NCES 2001-030). Washington, DC: US Department of Education, National Center for Education Statistics.

Mayor's Task Force on Hunger and Homelessness (2005). *Ten-Year plan to end chronic homelessness*. San Antonio, TX.

McGhee, P. (1971). Development of the humor response: A review of the literature. *Psychological bulletin*, 76. 328-348.

McGhee, P. (1989). The contribution of humor to children's social development. *Journal of children in contemporary society*, 20. 119-134.

McGhee, P. (1996). *Health, healing and the amuse system*. Dubuque, IA: Kendall Hunt Publishing Co.

McKinney-Vento homeless education assistance act of 2001. House Rule 1. Public Law 107-110. Signed into law 1/08/2002, effective 7/01/2002.

Mead, L. (1992). *New York Times*. May 19, 1992.

Medcalf Davenport, N.A. (2003). Questions, answers and wait-time: Implications for readiness testing of young children. *International journal of early years education, 11 (3), October, 2003*. Oxford, UK: Carfax Publishing. 245-253.

Molnar, J.M. (1990). Constantly compromised: The impact of homelessness on children. *Journal of social issues* 46(4). 109-124.

National Alliance to End Homelessness (2000). *A plan: Not a dream, How to end homelessness in ten years*. Washington, DC.

National Center for Education Statistics (1999). *Urban schools: The challenge of location and poverty.* Washington, DC: U.S. Department of Education, Institute of Education Sciences.

National Center for Education Statistics (2004). *The condition of education 2004.* Washington, DC: U.S. Department of Education, Institute of Education Sciences.

National Center for Homeless Education at SERVE (2005). *Homeless education: An introduction to the issues.* Greensboro, NC. Retrieved 10/7/05 from www.serve.org/nche/downloads/briefs/introduction.pdf.

National Center on Family Homelessness (1999). *Homeless children: America's new outcasts.* Newton, MA.

National Coalition for the Homeless (1989). *Homelessness in America: A summary.* New York, NY.

National Coalition for the Homeless (2001). *Homeless families with children.* Retrieved March 10, 2004 from http://www.nationalhomeless.org/families.html.

National Coalition for the Homeless (2003). *Illegal to be homeless: The criminalization of homelessness in the United States.* Washington, D.C.

National Coalition for the Homeless (2006a). *Education of homeless children and youth: NCH Fact Sheet #10.* Washington, DC. Retrieved 7/14/2006 from http://www.nationalhomeless.org/publications/education.pdf.

National Coalition for the Homeless (2006b). *How YOU can help end homelessness: NCH Fact Sheet #19.* Washington, DC. Retrieved 10/31/2006 from http://www.nationalhomeless.org/publications/facts/you.pdf.

National Commission on Teaching and America's Future (2003). *No dream denied: A pledge to America's children,* 10. Washington, DC: Children's Defense Fund Press.

National Foundation Advisory Group for Ending Homelessness (2000). *Ending homelessness: The philanthropic role.* Washington, DC.: Neighborhood Funders Group.

National Governors' Association (1992). *Every child ready for school: Report of the action team on school readiness* (Report No. ISBN-1-55877-155-7). Washington, DC: National Governors' Association Publications. (ERIC Document Reproduction Service No. ED 351 125).

National Research Council (2002). *Minority students in special and gifted education.* Washington, D.C.: National Academy Press, p 174.

Neisworth, J.T., & Bagnato, S.J. (1988). Assessment in early childhood special education. In Odom & Karnes (Eds.), *Early intervention for infants and children with handicaps,* Baltimore, MD: Brookes. 23-49.

Nicholls, J.G. (1989). *The competitive ethos and democratic education.* Cambridge, MA: Harvard University Press.

No Child Left Behind (2004). United States Government. Retrieved 8/15/06 from www.ed.gov/nclb/methods/teachers/hqtflexibility.html.

Nolen-Hoeksema, S.; Girus, J.S.; & Seligman, M.E.P. (1986). Learned helplessness in children: A longitudinal study of depression, achievement, and explanatory style. *Journal of personality and social psychology,* 51. 435-442.

Norwood, G. (2004). *Maslow's hierarchy of needs.* Retrieved 1/19/06 from http://www.deepermind.com/maslow.

O'Mara, D. (2004). *Providing access to verbal humor play for children with severe communication impairment.* unpublished doctoral thesis. Applied Computing Division, University of Dundee, Scotland. Retrieved 10/8/2004 from http://www.computing.dundee.ac.uk/staff/domara/home.asp.

O'Mara, D.; Waller, A.; Tait, L; Hood, H.; Booth, L.; & Brophy-Arnott, B. (2000). Developing personal identity through story telling. *IEE colloquium on speech and language processing for disabled and elderly people.* ISBN 0963-3308.

Outekhine, I. (1998). *Children's jokes: A developmental approach*. Paper presented at Imatra, Semiotic Symposium. St. Petersburg, Russia.

Partnership for Hope (1991). *Pride and Poverty, A Report on San Antonio*. San Antonio, TX.

Payne, R.K. (1998). *A Framework for understanding poverty (Revised edition)*. Baytown, TX: RFT Publishing Co.

Pellegrini, A.D. (2001). Practitioner review: The role of direct observation in the assessment of young children. *Journal of child psychology and psychiatry and allied disciplines*, 42(7). 861-869.

Pinnell, G.S. (1996). Ways to look at the functions of children's language. In Power and Hubbard (Eds.), *Language development, A reader for teachers*. Englewood Cliffs, NJ: Prentice-Hall, Inc.. 146-154.

Pinnell, G.S. (2001). Language in primary classrooms. *Theory into practice,14(5)*. 318-327.

Pinnell, G.S. & Matlin M.L. (Eds.) (1989). *Teachers and research, language learning in the classroom*. Newark, DE: International Reading Association.

Pressley, M.; Allington, R.L.; Wharton-MacDonald, R.; Collins-Black, C.; & Morrow, L. (2001). *Learning to read: Lessons for exemplary first-grade classrooms*. New York: Guilford.

Pressley, M. & Woloshyn, V. (1995). *Cognitive strategy instruction that really improves children's academic performance*, 2nd Ed. Cambridge, NH: Brookline Books.

Prince, D.L. & Howard, E.M. (2002). Children and their basic needs. *Early childhood education journal*, 30(1). 27-31.

Reed, S. & Sautter, R.C. (1992). Children of poverty. In Kraljic, M (Ed.) *The homeless problem*. The reference shelf, 64(2). New York, NY: The H.W. Wilson Company. 69-82.

Rogers, J. (1991). *Education report of rule 706*. Expert Panel presented in B.H. v. Johnson, 715 F. Supp. 1387. Illinois.

Rogoff, B. & Toma, C. (1997). Shared thinking: Community and institutional variations. *Discourse processes*. 471-497.

Rose, M. (1989). *Lives on the boundary*. New York, NY: Penguin Books.

Rubin, D. (2000). *Teaching elementary language arts: A balanced approach* (6th Ed.). Boston, MA: Allyn and Bacon. xxv.

San Antonio Express News (February 19, 2005). San Antonio, TX. 4D.

SAHA (2006). San Antonio Housing Authority information website. Retrieved on 10/27/2006 from http://www.saha.org/public%20housing/html/public_housing.html.

San Antonio Police Department (2005). Retrieved 2/4/05 from http://www.sanantonio.gov/sapd/DATA/CENTDATA0105.htm

Sanjek, R. (1990). On ethnographic validity. *Fieldnotes: The making of anthropology*. Ithaca, NY: Cornell University Press. 385-418.

Santos, F & Ingrassia, R. (2002). Family surge at shelters. *New York daily news*, August 18, 2002. Retrieved 3/10/04 from www.nationalhomeless.org/housing/familiesarticle.html.

Shaw, G.B. (1971). *The intelligent woman's guide to Socialism, Capitalism, Sovietism and Fascism*. Dublin, Ireland: Penguin Books. Retrieved 12/12/2006 from http://history.eNotes.com/famous-quotes/.

Shinn, M. & Weitzman, B. (1996). Predictors of homelessness among families in New York City: From shelter request to housing stability. *American journal of public health*, 88. 1651-1657.

Shonkoff, J.P. & Phillips, D.A. (Eds) and National Research Council and Institute of

Medicine Board on Children, Youth, and Families. Commission on Behavioral and Social Sciences Education (2000). *From neurons to neighborhoods: The science of early childhood development.* Washington, DC: National Academy Press.

Shultz, T.R. & Horibe, F. (1974). Development of the appreciation of verbal jokes. *Developmental psychology,* 10. 13-20.

Simeonsson, R.J., Huntington, G.S., & Parse, S.A. (1980). Assessment of children with severe handicaps: Multiple problems—multivariate goals. *Journal of the association for the severely handicapped,* 5(1). 55-72.

Simeonsson, R.J.; Huntington, G.S.; Short, R.J.; & Ware, W.B. (1982). The Carolina record of individual behavior: Characteristics of handicapped infants and children. *Topics in early childhood special education,* 2(2). 43-55.

Skinner, E.A.; Zimmer-Gembeck, M.J.; & Connell, J.P. (1998). Individual differences and the development of perceived control (254). *Monographs of the society for research in child development,* 63. 2-3.

Slavin, R.E. (1998). Can education reduce social inequity?. *Educational leadership.* 6-10.

Smith-Burke, M.T. (1985). Reading and talking: Learning through interaction. In Jaggar & Smith-Burke (Eds.), *Observing the language learner.* Newark, DE: International Reading Association and Urbana, IL: National Council of Teachers of English. 199-211.

Spector, C.C. (1990). Linguistic humor comprehension of normal and language impaired adolescents. *Journal of speech and hearing disorders,* 55. 533-541.

Stewart B. McKinney homeless assistance act (1987). First passed as PL 100-77 and named for U.S. Representative Stewart B. McKinney, Republican from Connecticut.

Taylor, B.M.; Peterson, D.S.; Pearson, P.D.; & Rodriguez, M. (2002). Looking inside classrooms: Reflecting on the 'how' as well as the 'what' in effective reading instruction. *The reading teacher,* 56. 70-79.

Taylor, D. & Dorsey-Gaines, C. (1988). *Growing up literate: Learning from inner-city families.* Portsmouth, NH: Heinemann.

Teale, W.H. (1986). Home background and young children's literacy development. In Teale and Sulzby (Eds.), *Emergent literacy:Writing and reading.* Norwood, NJ: Ablex.

Texas Center for Educational Research (2000). *The cost of teacher turnover.* Austin, TX. Retrieved 6/3/06 from http://www.tcer.org/publications/teacher_turnover_full.doc

Tough, J. (1977). *The development of meaning: A study of children's use of language.* London, England: Allen & Unwin.

Tsuchida, I. & Lewis, C. (1996). Responsibility and learning: Some preliminary hypotheses about Japanese elementary classrooms. In Rohlen & LeTender (Eds.), *Teaching and learning in Japan.* New York, NY: Cambridge University Press. 190-212.

United States Bureau of the Census (2001). *Poverty in the United States: Current population reports.* Washington, D.C.: Income Statistics Branch.

United States Conference of Mayors (2001). *A status report on hunger and homelessness in America's cities.* Washington, D.C.

United States Department of Education (2000). *Report to Congress: Barriers to education for the homeless.* Washington, DC.

Urban Institute (2000). *A new look at homelessness in America.* Washington, D.C. Retrieved 6/28/06 from www.urban.org

Vissing, Y. (1996). *Out of sight, out of mind: Homeless children and families in small town America.* Lexington, KY: The University Press of Kentucky.

Vygotsky, L.S. (1978). *Mind in society: The development of higher psychological processes.* Cambridge: Harvard University Press.

Waller, A. (1992). *Providing narratives in an augmentative communication system.* Unpublished doctoral thesis. Applied computing division, University of Dundee, Scotland.

Waller, A.; O'Mara, D.; Tait, L.; Hood, H.; Booth, L.; & Brophy-Arnott, B. (2001). Using written stories to support the use of narrative in conversational interaction: An AAC Case Study. *Augmentative and alternative communication,* 17. 221-232.

Wharton-McDonald, R. & Williamson, J. (2002). Focus on the real and make sure it connects to kids' lives. In Allington and Johnston (Eds.), *Reading to learn: Lessons from exemplary fourth-grade classrooms.* New York, NY: Guilford. 78-98.

Whitehurst, G.J. (1997). Language processes in context: Language learning in children reared in poverty. In Adamson & Romski (Eds.), *Communication and language acquisition: Discoveries from atypical development.* Baltimore, MD: Paul H. Brookes Publishing Co. 233-265.

Wolfgang, A. (1977). The silent language in the multicultural classroom. *Theory into practice, 16* (June). 145-157.

Wolfentein, M. (1978). *Children's humor.* South Bend IN: Indiana University Press.

Wright, J.D. (1989). *Address Unknown: The homeless in America.* Hawthorne, NY: Aldine de Gruyter Publishing Co.

www.homesforthehomeless.com

Young, R. (1992). *Critical theory and classroom talk.* Philadelphia, PA: Multilingual Matters.

Zeni, J. (1996). A picaresque tale from the land of kidwatching: Teacher research and ethical dilemmas. *The quarterly.* National Writing Project. Retrieved 5/31/06 from http://www.writingproject.org/cs/nwpp/lpt/nwpr/279.

Index

About the Author

Neva Ann Medcalf, Ed.D. is an Associate Professor of Education and Director of the Master of Arts in Reading program at St. Mary's University in San Antonio, Texas. She teaches both graduate and undergraduate students, supervises student teachers and interns, does extensive field experience in area schools, and provides professional development workshops for both public and private schools teachers. She directs a summer reading program for children in who come to the University campus, work with graduate students to strengthen their reading skills, and to use those skills in the study of Earth Science. She serves on the Board of Directors and is Chair of Professional Devleopment for the Achievers Center for Excellence, a secondary school for students with special needs. She is active at University United Methodist Church, teaching a Sunday School class for adults, helping with the children's music ministry, and volunteering for service in programs for the homeless such as the SAMM shelter.

Dr. Medcalf is the author of numerous articles regarding the language development of children, the testing of young children, and the uses of technology in training future teachers.

Dr. Medcalf's daughter, Morrisa Booker, son-in-law, Cpt. Erik L. Booker, four grandsons, Alex, Brennan, Colton and Devin, are stationed in Germany. Her son, Eric Medcalf, lives in San Antonio.